MW00931477

Think & Date Like A Man

Think & Date Like A Man

✦

(Be the woman who gets the man she wants… and keeps him!)

April Masini

Nicknamed "The New Millennium's Dear Abby" by the media,

Author of the critically acclaimed

'Ask April' advice column, AskApril.com, online magazine &

Best-selling book "Date Out Of Your League"

iUniverse, Inc.

New York Lincoln Shanghai

Think & Date Like A Man
(Be the woman who gets the man she wants...and keeps him!)

Copyright © 2005 by Masini Enterprises, Inc

All rights reserved. No part of this book may be used or reproduced by any means, graphic, electronic, or mechanical, including photocopying, recording, taping or by any information storage retrieval system without the written permission of the publisher except in the case of brief quotations embodied in critical articles and reviews.

iUniverse books may be ordered through booksellers or by contacting:

iUniverse
2021 Pine Lake Road, Suite 100
Lincoln, NE 68512
www.iuniverse.com
1-800-Authors (1-800-288-4677)

ISBN-13: 978-0-595-37466-3 (pbk)
ISBN-13: 978-0-595-81860-0 (ebk)
ISBN-10: 0-595-37466-2 (pbk)
ISBN-10: 0-595-81860-9 (ebk)

Printed in the United States of America

Contents

Section III: The Bedroom

Introduction

Think & Date Like a Man is not for the faint-of-heart, the easily embarrassed, or ladies wanting a feel-good session. It's direct, refreshingly real, and at times, down and dirty, just like actual relationships with men! Think & Date Like a Man is for women who are ready to hear the bold, honest, and often times brutal truth, about how and what men—and not just any men, but the most successful and wealthy men—think about women. But that's just the tip of the dating iceberg.

In this tell-all book, April Masini will take you on a step-by-step journey turning you into that exciting and elusive woman that successful and powerful men want. And if anyone would know, it's April. She has dated (and married!) some of the most successful, wealthy, and famous A-List men. Now she wants to show you how you can, too!

Think & Date Like a Man is a combination of April's professional and personal expertise and experiences, her philosophies and strategies, along with her trade-mark humor and lots of juicy dating tidbits about the world of high-level dating. You'll find revealing insights into the minds of successful, rich, and powerful men, while uncovering the secret to attracting, captivating, and keeping them. After reading this book, you will know so much about thinking and dating like a man that you'll become the dating guru to every single woman who knows you. And the best part is you'll be so confident in yourself that you'll never give a second thought to revealing these tips to "the competition." You can't ask for much more from a book than that—unless you're interested in her other books:

1) Date Out Of Your League is for men only, and it shows men how to succeed with women by knowing what it is that women really want—not just what men have been led to believe they want. While you can peek if you must, it's really a great gift for any man you care about who's run up against a myriad of the wrong kinds of women, the lunacy and worse than any of that—no dates at all.

2) 50 First Dates tells you how to romance your date and create dates that can make all the difference between sizzle and splat. April goes into detail and gives

you 50 dates that you can take your honey on to guarantee romance. This book takes the anxiety and the work out of dating, and lets you enjoy the sex and romance that comes naturally when everything else is in place.

3) The Next 50 Dates is the sequel to 50 First Dates because after 50 dates, you need to make sure that your momentum doesn't wane. This book tells you how to keep the allure in your dating, your long-term relationship or your marriage. It's got 50 more great ideas for sexy, exciting dates. Read it as a how to guide or as an inspirational jumping off point—but read it if you're in a relationship and you want to keep the spice hot.

Think & Date Like A Man was written in response to the overwhelming number of questions and letters of concern April received from readers' and fans' about men, dating and relationships—specifically, "April, no matter what I do, I just can't seem to meet and date (much less marry) the kind of man I want. Would you please help me? What am I doing wrong?"

Ladies, you asked April how to attract and 'close the deal' with Mr. Right, and April wrote Think & Date Like A Man to tell you how.

We all know that men differ from women in so many ways, especially in how they think—in this case, how they think about women, about sex, about dating, and about relationships. Now, if you were trying to make a business deal with, say, a Japanese CEO, wouldn't it make sense to learn how the Japanese think and speak? Attracting a man is no different than scoring a successful deal: You want something from (or better, with) him—a relationship. Mastering the intricacies of the mind of your prospective mate is the key to attaining him—and keeping him. So learn his language. Learn his thought processes. And be prepared for success: That understanding will greatly increase your odds of getting what you want.

Here's an example: Unlike a woman, a man does not worship at the altar of The Relationship. He does not throw himself body and soul into developing and nurturing The Relationship. He does not fall apart like a house of cards if The Relationship doesn't work out. It's not that a relationship wouldn't be important to him at some point down the line. And it's not that he can't commit or isn't capable of real love. It's just that The Relationship isn't the be-all and end-all of his existence.

What is the be-all and end-all of a man's life? He is. His needs, his desires, and his goals are. Men were not brought up to please everyone around them like most women were. Men have been doted on and waited on by over attentive mothers since birth. While girls were learning how to make boys happy, boys were learning how to make themselves happy. As a result, men have learned that THEY are the center of the universe. Not you. Not the relationship. Does this mean that men will never want a relationship? Of course it doesn't. A relationship with you could very well be on a man's list of desires. But if it is, it's probably not his only desire or even the most important one to him. On the list of things important in his life, getting to know you could be ranked number 3, 7, or 12, along with his career, exercising, sports, his male friends, his family, his female friends, his hobbies, his penis, his quest to find himself, his search for an autographed photo of Angelina Jolie on eBay, or even his desire to simply be alone for a while.

And just as you are hopefully on his list of life essentials, you are certainly not the only one on that list. To men, dating is a numbers game. He's not waiting by the phone for you to call. He's not planning his weekend around you and your schedule. He's getting out there, increasing the odds—his odds—at least, for now. At least, until you both have mutually made that agreement of exclusivity. Until then, he's not marrying you, he's not getting engaged to you, he's not committing to you; he is dating. He is dating you, just like he is dating other women. He's finding out what's out there, what he likes, what he needs. That's what a man does. That's how a man thinks. That's how a man dates. And that's what you should do, how you should think, and how you should date—if you hope to eventually have that mutual commitment. Because if he gets wind of your worship at the altar of The Relationship before he's even considered what's between the two of you, he'll be out the door.

Think & Date Like a Man will reveal how a man thinks and dates so that knowing this, you can now employ your most womanly powers effectively.

Man-Think Self Assessment Quiz

Now that you know why it's important to Think & Date Like a Man, it's time to see how close to, or how far away from that you really are. If you're like most women, you'll find that your Woman-Think and his Man-Think are on polar ends of the earth. Answer the next 10 questions with total honesty, and I'll help you determine how sharp your Man-Think skills are and how much fine-tuning you need to Think and Date Like Man.

1. What do guys dislike doing most on a date?
   a. Going to the ballet.
   b. Going clothing shopping.
   c. Talking about where The Relationship is heading.
   d. Being asked about their past relationships.

2. How do you know if a guy really likes you?
   a. He brings you flowers.
   b. He courts you with gifts and restaurant meals.
   c. He introduces you to his friends.
   d. He tells you.

3. What does it mean when a guy has sex with you?
   a. He loves you.
   b. He's ready for an exclusive relationship with you and only you.
   c. He's attracted to you and you were willing.
   d. He wants to have children.

4. When should you suggest your date cancel his sports event to be with you?
   a. When you're really serious about him.
   b. When your parents are available to meet him.
   c. When you're lonely and miss being with him so much.
   d. When you're about to give birth to his child.

5. What kind of a surprise does a guy like most?
    a. When he comes to pick you up for a date and you open the door nude.
    b. When you show up at his workplace with a home-cooked meal and flowers.
    c. When you show up at his home completely unexpected.
    d. When you suddenly burst into tears because you're so happy being with him.

6. When will a guy ask you to marry him?
    a. On your 6-month anniversary.
    b. If and when he feels you're The One.
    c. On your one year anniversary.
    d. Trick question—you should propose to him.

7. What's the best thing to say when you first see a guy's place?
    a. "I like your place."
    b. "Cleaning lady's year off?"
    c. "If we're gonna be together, some of this stuff has got to go."
    d. "This place has everything but a velvet painting of dogs playing poker."

8. What do you tell your date when an extremely attractive woman walks by?
    a. "How could anyone wear a dress like that? What a whore!"
    b. "Jeez, why don't you take a picture? It lasts longer."
    c. "Wow, she's really pretty."
    d. "You're not attracted to someone like that, are you?"

9. What is a guy's primary goal in asking you out for a date?
    a. He wants to get married and have children with you.
    b. He wants to see you naked.
    c. He wants to find out about your hopes, plans, and dreams.
    d. He wants to show you off to his friends and family.

10. Which of the following is a relationship deal-breaker for a guy?
    a. A woman who's a few extra pounds overweight.
    b. A woman who prefers waiting until marriage to have sex.
    c. A woman who has children.
    d. A woman who still lives with her parents.

Quiz Answers

1. [C] While ballet, clothing shopping, and past relationship talk are about as much fun for a guy as getting a root canal, bringing up where The Relationship is heading is like getting that same root canal—without the anesthesia.

2. [D] Oh, sure—flowers, gifts, meals, and friends are nice, but guys are pretty straight—forward. Chances are if they care for you, you'll hear about it. And you just can't put a price on "I like you."

3. [C] When a guy has sex with you, it means he's attracted to you and you were willing. Period. I take that back—he may or may not be attracted to you. It means he's horny and you were willing. Are guys that shallow? Hmmm, let me think...yes.

4. [D] Suggest a guy cancel his sports event to be with you only when you're about to give birth to his child, and even then, think twice about it. Certain things are holy to guys—beer, cars, and sports. You're not there yet. He'll let you know when you are.

5. [A] Never show up at his workplace or home; God knows what state he'll be in or who'll be with him. And tears of happiness at this stage are just psycho. For a classic, all-American, always-in-good-taste surprise, you just can't beat unexpected nudity.

6. [B] If you chose "D," you need way more help than this book can offer.

7. [A] Insulting a guy's place is one step away from laughing at his penis. Once you've been together for a while, you can start making subtle suggestions. Until then, keep your eyes closed and your arms open.

8. [C] Saying a pretty woman's pretty is just affirming what your guy is already thinking. Plus, it shows you're secure and it's a great set-up for him to follow up with a compliment—something like, "Almost as pretty as you." See? She did you a favor!

9. [B] Every guy who asks you out wants to see you naked. You can either let that bother you, or be flattered by it. Don't blame him; that's how guys are wired.

10. [B] Let's be honest—you could be a leper, but if you're having great sex with your guy, he's enjoying the relationship. Now, while there's nothing wrong with wanting to wait till marriage to have sex, that's your right—just don't expect the guy to wait with you. He's already thinking about that other woman who's far less patient than you are.

What kind of Man-Think skills are you starting out with?

9–10 Correct Answers: You're an Advanced Man-Thinker. You've got the basics down, and now it's time to turn all that thinking into scoring your perfect match. Go get 'em brainiac!

5–8 Correct Answers: You're an Intermediate Man-Thinker. You're on the right track, but you still have a way to go to master the mind of the dating man. Read on and we'll have you fine-tuned and in the dating rotation in no time.

0–4 Correct Answers: You're an Amateur—A Beginner Man-Thinker. For the love of God, immediately cease dating until you're done reading this book! But have no fear—there is hope for you yet!

Section I:
The War Room

This book is a direct result of thousands of letters, questions and complaints I have received from women through my column, Ask April, and my website, AskApril.com—specifically, the whining and complaining about wanting (but failing) to get married, and if not that, from women who were in love and were left. Interestingly enough, both groups sing the same tune: I'm really lonely and really afraid, suffering from low self-esteem, filled with self doubt and consumed with insecurity and lack of confidence. Help me!

This book will (hopefully) take you on a journey from whiner to winner and help you to think less like Princess Diana, and more like Camilla Parker Bowles—the woman who didn't look like a princess at first glance, but got the prince, hook line and sinker, at the end of the story. Diana was sweet and good—but hopelessly and helplessly sad in love. Camilla, however, used her skills to get her prince. She was not more beautiful than Diana—in fact she was way less so. She was not younger than Diana. She was older. But despite the supposed disadvantages of youth and beauty, Camilla had what it took to get what she wanted, and that is why she is a good example of what I want to impart to you, that you do not have to be the most beautiful woman in the room to get the man you want—or to get all the men in the room, for that matter. What you do have to be is wise.

Yes, we are living in modern times, and cyber dating is a virtual reality, but don't be fooled. Men seek in women the same thing that they did thousands of years ago—their yearnings and desires have not changed. What has changed is that the Feminist Movement has given us bad advice and told us what we supposedly want, and what men supposedly want. The media has augmented that bad advice, and many people have believed them. But I'm here to tell you, don't believe the Feminist hype, and ignore the media—they're wrong.

The truth is this, ladies: Men still want 'to see stars' when they fall in love; they want to feel 'butterflies in their stomachs,' they want fireworks exploding and they want to be 'carried away' by the most captivating, alluring, enchanting, mesmerizing, fascinating seductress ever—a woman who completely bewitches. Men want to yearn. Desire is like a drug—in fact, it is a drug! But you can't buy it. Not even illegally! However, I will teach you to elicit it and use it to your advantage.

I will show you how a man thinks and dates, but I will also acknowledge and tip my hat to the courtesans, geishas, and women of other eras who took seduction seriously. We have just as much to learn from them, as we do from men.

Not since the courtesans of Europe and the geishas of Japan, has anyone specialized in men or been so valued for their powers of seduction of men. These women earned titles that didn't include Mrs., but did include Goddess and Seductress, because of their knowledge of the art of captivating men. Don't get me wrong. This is not about sluts and whores who are paid money for a night of pleasure. (It's not too hard to have sex with a man.) These were women with self esteem and rich lives, who made their livings and their lives by knowing and practicing enticement and seduction in long relationships with men, not by trapping them, but by enchanting them with a working arsenal of talents, skills and education that kept men wanting more. Manslayers vary in the way they look, or in the way they dress, or even in the era they are born into, but their basic modus operandi remains (for the most part) the same. No, these are not women who feel they are nothing and no one, without a man—are you kidding? These are women who love men, but don't need a man. And what a wonderful state for a woman to be in—wanting, but not needing. It is how you will make the wisest decisions in your life when it comes to relationships. You will not be left for another women—in fact, if anyone does the leaving, it will be you.

These goddesses—the women for whom men give up thrones and fortunes, went to war, and fought duels to the death—are powerful in ways most cannot fathom.... Yet, behind the black magic may lurk a somewhat 'average' or 'plain' looking woman. And yet, time and again, she will beat out the most beautiful of competitors through her sheer will, her commanding presence, her dominate confidence, and her grand standing, look at me attitude...although it may be subtle (at first) she sends forth very powerful and provocative psychological messages.

So, as you read about the way men think and date, and consider what it is you've been thinking and doing in dating until now, think about some new mantras for yourself: Enchantress, vixen, seductress, siren, enticer, vamp...

1

What Men Think About Love

I don't know why women want any of the things that men have when one of the things women have is men.

—Coco Chanel

OK, now that you've taken the little quiz and know how much you do (or don't) think like a man, I'm going to let you in on a little secret…Men see dating, as they do life, as sales. That is a fact. You may not like it, you may not agree with it, you may not even want to believe it, but you better start accepting it, because it is the way it is. So, if you want to think like a man does, then it's time to get to know your audience and to understand the consumer—in your case, men. If you follow the three basic rules to success in sales, you'll have more insight into what goes on in their mind:

• Rule #1—Know and understand your consumer.
• Rule #2—Give them what they want.
• Rule #3—Analyze the competition and do things better than they do.

So, that's what the men are doing. Only somewhere along the line, we got the Feminist message that we should do that, too. So we started phoning men, asking them out on dates, paying for dinner, making the first move and even proposing marriage—or worse—moving in together. And it seemed okay, only as time went on, it became clear that what we had on our hands was a disaster. Never have there been more divorces, unhappy relationships and singles desperate to be in relationships.

A while ago, a group of women asked me if a woman should ever propose to a man. At that moment, it hit me—the Feminist Movement has given us women some bad advice. I told that group of women not to listen to the traditional Feminist Movement when it comes to matters of the heart. In terms of dating and love, men and women are on opposite ends of the spectrum. We've always been this way and we always will be. Evolution has not shown changes in these roles. Ever.

There have been many advances in the rights of women over the years—they've resulted in higher wages, more opportunities, and all sorts of freedoms women had never experienced before. But a funny thing happened when women started knocking down all the office walls that once stalled their careers: We started knocking down the bedroom walls as well…. with some disastrous results!

Confused as to what you should do? Let me help straighten it all out for you.

Snap out of it! Unlearn what the Feminists Taught Us:
* Don't ask men out.
* Don't initiate phone calls to men.
* Don't give a man your phone number if he hasn't asked for it.
* And DON'T ASK A MAN TO MARRY YOU!

Although the feminist movement would have had us believe otherwise, men and women are different. Sometimes complete opposites of each other. And nowhere are these differences more evident than when it comes to amore. Sure, we may all be looking for someone with whom to spend our lives, but how men and women go about finding that love is as different as night and day or apples and oranges. You get the picture.

The good news is that men do need commitment (at some point in their lives) just as much as women do—but they want it packaged differently. When people write to me asking if they ever will find their "soul mates", I tell them that they have to change their thinking processes. Our male soul mates will not be the same as us; we are not looking for our twin. Men are coming from a completely different place and traveling in a whole different mode of transportation. If you don't quite get why we're so different and why we have to respect those differences, read on! You'll be shocked to discover how different love is for men and women.

> *I used to believe that marriage would diminish me, reduce my options. That you had to be someone less to live with someone else when, of course, you have to be someone more.*
> —Candice Bergen

• FORGET about implementing "total disclosure" when you first meet a man, and forget about being completely up-front, honest, and open about what you are thinking and feeling.

First of all, you want to create mystery. You want him to want to know more about you. In fact, you want him to want to know everything about you. If you tell him all there is up front, he'll be sated, and that's no good for allure! Second, too much information can be a real mood-killer. Although it may sound great in theory, in the dating arena, the "over-share" will not only prove ineffective, it will probably send the man running in the opposite direction. He doesn't need to know everything right away—because he doesn't want to know everything right away. Men do not have the same need to really "know" one another's deepest darkest secrets. Ladies, as much as you want the man in your life to want to know all about you (so he can "understand the real you")—the feeling is not mutual. Sorry, but that is a misconception…I strongly advise against stressing yourself out in the pursuit of searching his soul. If he doesn't offer, don't dig. All he really wants to do is desire you. He wants to feel great, and he wants to know you do, too. He wants to show you a good time on a date that you can both enjoy. Period.

* FORGET about being too available.

He wants to chase you. If he gets you too easily, you'll have denied him the chase he wants. He doesn't want to feel like he got the booby prize date that doesn't have anything else going on, and is lucky to have something to do. He wants to feel lucky he got the date.

* FORGET about accepting last minute dates.

Again, he may want you tonight (or tomorrow night), but he'll want you even more if you're already busy. He'll realize that to get you, he's going to have to fend off other suitors. It sounds old fashioned, but it's true. When he does get you on a date, he'll be more excited about it.

* FORGET about making the first move.

Let the man be the aggressor and the pursuer. Don't you dare lean in to kiss him on the first date or on your second date, either. In fact, don't make it too easy for him to kiss you—or more. Hugh Grant was speaking for 99% of men when he said he misses the 'chase' as a reason for going to a hooker, when he had the beautiful Ms. Hurley home alone in bed. Ladies, this is the real life—not a movie where men are tender heart romantics who never judge a woman who sleeps with them too soon. Yes, when presented with the opportunity most men will have sex, although there are always exceptions—they probably won't pursue a long-term romance with what they see as an easy woman. Sounds harsh, I know, but deep down they feel she's decreased her 'value'.

Factoid: Women need a reason to have sex. Men just need a place.

---

* FORGET about calling men "just to talk."

Your job is to create mystery, allure and desire. If you are too available, and if you don't give him the opportunity to miss you, you'll lose the tension you are trying to build. The only reason for calling a man is to return his call. Period.

* FORGET about telling a man you like him first.

Let a man express his feelings and interest first. Let him feel the sheer terror of not being sure that you will accept his feelings or even return them. Believe it or not, this is part of the adrenalin rush he craves when he chases women. It may seem cruel, but if so, it's because you don't understand his needs. The more uncertainty and terror he feels, the greater the conquest, when you return his feelings. Remember—you're not his mother. It's not your job to make him feel safe. You are there to make him keep coming back.

* FORGET about stressing over petty details. He doesn't care!

He's not your girlfriend—he's a man. He's not going to care or even notice if your handbag is "a little bit off" or if you're a brunette and he's always had a thing for blondes. Quit making yourself crazy. He doesn't care about that stuff. You're out on a date with a great guy. Besides, here's how your "obsessions" are probably playing out in his head:

She didn't exactly come across as brilliant, but she sure blew my mind whenever we kissed. She snores when she sleeps, but she sleeps naked. She can't keep her mouth shut, but she loves oral sex. I can hear her pee, but as soon as she comes out of the bathroom, she'll ride me like a wild Bronco. She's on her period, but as soon as it's over, we'll have sex again. Actually, on second thought…why wait?

Are you starting to see the pattern? Of course, that's at the beginning of the relationship. As time goes on, those things, even the ones that he actually told you he considers cute, will come to be perceived as less cute, and more annoying. This process is directly proportional to the amount of sex you're having, or not having. The ratio is: The more sex you have, the longer he'll consider those things cute (or at least not annoying). Cut back on the sex and suddenly your snoring will be perceived as cannon fire, and all that cute talking you do? Good grief, can't she ever give that mouth a rest (or at least figure out something better to do with it)?

And take heart, while men might not worry as much about their weight, or what they said (or didn't say) as much as women do, they do have their own concerns…penis size (shape, girth, etc.) being chief among them, with hair loss, height, and job position (success level) coming in next. The reality is, men worry and obsess, too—just about different things.

> *If the world were a logical place, men would ride sidesaddle.*
> —Rita Mae Brown

* FORGET about cheating on him.

Men look for loyalty in a woman, and while "Stand by Your Man" may have been a hit for Tammy Wynette—to say nothing of the long list of women who have made it their mantra over the years, from Hillary Rodham Clinton to Mary Jo Buttafuoco—don't think for one minute a man will begin singing the same tune! Men will not forgive a cheating girlfriend. Guys that have been betrayed, especially in the bedroom, are far less likely to forgive their partners than women would be in the same situation. Women can win big points by supporting their man in front of colleagues and friends and defending him when necessary.

Apply Your Understanding of These Differences

Let's go back to the question about whether a woman should ask a man for his hand in marriage. If you understand the male and female thought processes outlined above, you'll know that proposing to a man goes against his whole purpose of being—and ours too. Here's how the teachings from above should help you understand why you won't ever ask a man for marriage:

1. All Is Fair in Love and War
You are different on the inside and out. If you ask him to marry you, the true women in you will always wonder if he really loves you. Try and deny that you haven't dreamed of receiving your marriage proposal since you were a child. You have. Because you asked him, doubts will always plague your soul: Would he really rather be with someone else? After all he never asked you to marry him—you asked him. A man wants to be the one to propose. He just may not be ready. Don't take the opportunity away from him.

2. Honesty Schmonesty
If you ask a man to marry you, he doesn't have to win you—he has not won anything—you, in fact, have made him the prize! And you will, more likely than not, pay for it in the long run. Be the prize. Let him reach up to that pedestal to try and win you. Let him worry that you won't accept. When you finally do, he will have won more because of the adrenalin rush you created and gave him.

3. Stand by Your Man
Part of being loyal is in understanding our fundamental needs as different species. You have to be loyal not only to him, but to his raw wiring. If you try to assume the masculine role in love, think of it as cheating on his nuts and bolts. Don't take out the garbage, and don't ask him on out on a date, let alone propose to him. Let him be the man who does the "man things" around the house as well as socially and sexually.

Wrapping up!

Let me very clear about this: I do not think the woman should ever, ever, ever ask a man to get married. (Or ask him on a date, or call him on the telephone to chat or make the first move.)

> *If you want to get rid of a man, I suggest saying, "I love you, I want to marry you, I want to have your children." Sometimes they leave skid marks.*
>
> —Rita Rudner

If a woman feels like her guy is wasting her time and may never ask her to marry him, she should stop spending all of her time with him and immediately begin to date other men—period. Remember—let him do the chasing, not the other way around. If he loves her, he will come after her, he will try to win her back and he will ask her to marry him. If he doesn't, he doesn't love her enough to commit to spending his life with her. And why would anyone want to be with someone who does not love you? Next!

INTERESTING STATISTICS

Where and how to meet people:

With the exception of those who have never dated respondents surveyed cited the following as the top 3 ways of meeting people:

1. Through friends/family (65%)
2. School (51%)
3. Work (49%)

In an additional survey:
31% met their dates from a Night Club or Happy Hour
20% from a place of worship (church, synagogue, mosque, etc.),
19% went on a blind date
14% met via on-line chatting.

© E-Poll / Bridge Entertainment, Inc. All Rights Reserved.

2

Men And Their Biological Clocks

✦

—Yes, They Have Them, Too!
Learn What Makes Him Tick,
And Then You'll Really Know What Time It Is.

> *By all means marry; if you get a good wife, you'll be happy. If you get a bad one, you'll become a philosopher.*
> —Socrates (469 BC–399 BC)

It takes more than roping him in to tie the knot!

Men and marriage—what does it take to get the two together? If you're trying to get your boyfriend to make a commitment, I have good news and bad news. The good news is that you can stop trying to manipulate, sweet-talk or pressure him into proposing. The bad news is that there's nothing you can do to speed up the process. That's not to say it'll never happen. Men fall in love and get married every day. But men have their own biological clocks. When they're ready, they head down the aisle—but not a moment sooner. In the meantime, it's not possible to convince a commitment-phobic guy that you're the best thing that will ever happen to him—even if you are! Instead, your best bet is to look for someone who doesn't need convincing.

The Sex and the City gang once compared a marriage-ready man to a taxi: At a certain point in his life, he becomes ready for commitment. His "available" light goes on and the next lady in his life gets the ring. Luckily for us, it's easy to tell the difference between men who've got a light on and one who's just driving around in the dark. How can you tell the taxi light has gone on?

There's a new biological clock out there—the one ticking inside bachelors. After decades in which men statistically had the upper hand in the dating world, the demographics have reversed: For a big chunk of the dating pool, people ages 30 to 44, the number of single men and women are now about even, or in some cases, slightly tipped in women's favor. The odds are especially dismal for men looking for younger mates: By 2010, according to the U.S. Census Bureau, men in their late 30s and early 40s will out number women five to 10 years younger by two to one.

—The Wall Street Journal

How to spot a man who is ready for the whole enchilada:

1. A Man Who Wants To Become Your Husband Acts Like Your Husband.
When a man is ready to become a husband—your husband—he simply starts acting like a husband. For instance, he will talk about the future and he will make plans for the future; he will introduce you to his family and friends; he will not only call you daily, but he'll want to tell you the details of his day, while having a desire to hear about yours. Simply put, a man that wants to get married acts like he wants to get married.

On the other hand, a man who is not ready to get married behaves like a guy you are dating—meaning one of the guys you are dating. And if your guy's own version of the biological clock isn't telling him it's time to commit, there's absolutely no point in pushing him. You can make the mistake of giving him an ultimatum (as many women do), make promises about how great you'll be to him, and even ultimately snag him, but I guarantee he'll only end up resenting you for it, or worse—cheating or leaving. As soon as there's the first bump in the road, he'll point to the pressure you applied, with a "See, I knew I wasn't ready" retort. Please remember, it is absolutely imperative that a man feels he has to "win a woman"—he has to pursue her and he must ask her to marry him on his own volition, when he feels the time is right.

> *Men don't feel the urge to get married as quickly as women do because their clothes all button and zip in the front. Women's dresses usually button and zip in the back. We need men emotionally and sexually, but we also need men to help us get dressed.*
>
> —Rita Rudner

2. He Suggests You Would Have Beautiful Children

True, his clock does not tick with an alarm signaling the absolute deadline like the one that ends women's childbearing years. Just take a look at notable fathers like Tony Randall, Yasser Arafat, George Plimpton, Anthony Quinn, Clint Eastwood, Strom Thurmond and so many more have demonstrated that men can father babies no matter how old they get. While fertility doesn't decrease as dramatically for a man as it does for a woman, a man does have a biological clock, experts say. But these scientists disagree on exactly when the alarm sounds. In general, "there's a decline in testosterone of about 1% per year for men after age 30," said Dr. Harry Fisch, director of the Male Reproductive Center at Columbia University in New York City. But it's difficult to pinpoint which men will have trouble conceiving a child with a birth defect based on age, he said. "The problem is the biological clock ticks at different speeds for different men."

One sure clue that a man is ready for marriage is when he stares longingly at kids and suggests you would have beautiful children together. Most men want to be young enough to teach their sons to fish and play ball. Age can have a great effect on a man's attitude toward marriage. Most college-educated men don't consider marriage as a serious possibility until after age 26. In fact, they enter a phase of high commitment between the ages of 28 and 33. Men who've gone on to graduate school—doctors, lawyers, etc.—hit their commitment-peak phase during ages 30 to 36.

In a survey of 121 men in their 40s who were marrying for the first time, their reason for marrying was different than that of the younger men interviewed. Many of these older men were eager to marry because their biological clock was running. Obviously, a man's biological clock isn't the same as a woman's, but men are often in just as much of a hurry to have children. They're not worried about physically being able to father a child, but about being a father to the child. These surveyed men, 42 and older, who were about to marry looked forward to having children, and said that they almost unanimously pictured themselves as fathers of sons, and they wanted to be young enough when their sons came along to teach them all the things fathers traditionally teach their sons-to ride a bicycle, to pitch a tent camping, and so forth. The most important reason these men had for marrying was that if they waited much longer, they wouldn't be able to be active fathers. So if you meet a man in his forties who tells you he's eager to have a son so he can do those male-bonding things, know that these things are very important to him, and they'll dramatically increase his readiness to marry.

3. He's Financially Independent
Most men's priorities tend to be focused on winning financial security before having a family. If he's still struggling to pay his bills, he's not going to want to add the burden of supporting a wife. Moreover, if you're dealing with a man who is unable to commit to a full time job, he's not a good bet for a full time commitment to a marriage to you.

However, there is also the phenomenon of the man who has good job security, and indeed, is financially independent, yet still not able to leave the starting gate. Many very ambitious man have something called "the number"…that's the goal they are trying to reach financially, whether its half a million dollars, ten million dollars, or whatever. Though by any standard, they already have the financial means, psychologically, they still are not ready. They won't be ready until they hit that number, whatever it is for them.

> *All good things come to he who waits…As long as he works like hell while he waits!*
>
> —Philine van Lidth de Jeude

There is also a kind of man who is really married to his job. He tells everyone he is ready to meet the right woman, yet his priority is clearly work, and it has been for so long he is in sort of a rut. When he says, "he's ready," but the words don't match his actions—he doesn't call, he cancels dates, etc. you know he's got a Mrs. in his work. As a rule, stay away from any man who is a "project" for you. How do you know he's a project? As soon as you find yourself saying, "He really wants to be with me and spend more time with me BUT he's too busy/his mother is sick/his job is insane/he's too hurt from the last relationship/he's afraid"…. or any number of reasons (excuses) you've got a man on your hands who is not ready for marriage.

I'm not saying don't give a busy man slack. A busy, successful and powerful man IS busy…and he will want to know that you can roll with the punches of his schedule. If you want to be with a successful man, that is part of the bargain. But you should look for these clues: when there is a break in the schedule, he'll want to spend time with you. He'll want to touch base, even if he can't get together. He will respect you and communicate with you, even if he can't give you the prime slot.

A man can look like he has everything it takes to get married, and indeed, he can give lip service to the idea of getting married and be very attracted to you personally. He can tell you how special you are and mean it. Yet at the end of the day, he still may not be able to do it. For our purposes, it doesn't matter if a man doesn't want to do it, or if he wants to but can't do it. The man you want is one whose actions match his words. Having said that, it may take more than a few dates to figure this out, and you have to be patient.

4. He's Not Seduced By The Single's Scene Anymore

The fact is the singles scene no longer appeals to a man who is ready to marry. Men ready to commit, no matter what age they are, will freely admit to feeling uncomfortable and out of place in the bars, pool halls and dance clubs that were once their favorite pick up hotspots and hangouts. They will increasingly change their lifestyle to one that is more domestic, whether it is at their house, their married friends or their families. They might even leave that swinging loft downtown, and buy something in a good school system, with a yard.

These men tend to have interests and hobbies beyond "getting laid." They like taking walks, reading new books, learning, spending time with friends and family. All of these things are more interesting than hitting the latest, hip hangout. They don't always travel with a pack of buddies, and will go to coffee shops or the movies alone if they feel like it. If you're with a guy who is exhibiting these qualities, has financial independence, as well as shows you respect and interest, you may have found your man!

INTERESTING STATISTICS:

According to an AARP magazine survey: "Close to a third of unmarried, American women ages 40 through 60, who date, are going out with younger men."

Sex on a first date? Only 2 percent of single women in the age group approved, while 20 percent of the men were amenable.

Frequency of sex? Sixty percent of the women and 45 percent of the men surveyed said they hadn't had any in the past six months."

* Sixty percent of singles aged 40–69 are women, a majority of them divorced.
* Forty-two percent of the men and 24 percent of the women surveyed had never been married.
* Thirty-four percent of women say they're dating younger men—among the men, 66 percent said they were dating younger women.
* For both men and women, the top reason for dating was to find fun and companionship.
* Only 11 percent of the men and 2 percent of the women cited sex as the main motive.
* Eight percent of the respondents said they were dating in order to find a marriage partner
* Nine percent said they were looking for someone to live with.
* Thirty percent of the singles reported difficulty in finding dates. Many were attending mixers and using online dating services.

3

Dating Is About Sales

✦

Sales Is A Numbers Game
Play To Win

Men don't make passes at girls who wear glasses.
—Dorothy Parker
(If you don't know who Dorothy Parker is, start learning from
women of all generations. The more knowledge of
womankind you have, the more successful you'll be.)

Suppose for a moment that you eliminate all of the intangible woman-fluff that traditionally accompanies dating—in other words, take away romance and fate so that you're left with a pragmatic, practical point of view. I call this approach "The Numbers Game." It is based on the way men think about dating and business. If you get down to business and follow "The Numbers Game," it will save you hours of time, heartache and (a big red-flag to men!) over-analyzing. It will multiply your success in dating (or in just about anything else you do)—that is if you are willing to at least give it a try. You'll find that it can change your life. Let it.

The principles of the game:
1. You are a company.
2. You are the company's only salesman, marketer and advertiser.
3. Men are your company's customers and they make their buying decisions based upon the goods you produce (i.e. yourself); in other words, you have to present the best product with not only the best structural quality, but also the best packaging, and advertising possible. (You must have the best possible inner and outer selves.)
4. Your personal style differentiates your company from all the others. If you're going to compete in the Fortune 500, you'd better know how to generate the best revenue.

5. The world's best salesmen don't have a 100% sales rate, or a 75% sales rate; nor do they have a 50% sales rate, or even a 25% sales rate. The world's best salesmen are lucky to maintain a 10% sales rate. A 10% sales rate = one in every ten.

If you're not catching my drift yet, think of it this way: To win this game, you have to be the best company you can be, making the best product and selling the best services. Moreover, you have to keep trying to improve every aspect of your corporation, no matter what hurdles you face. (For example, the GAP went through a slow sales period for some years, but the company has started posting increases in their quarterly sales.)

Need another example for how to play The Numbers Game, other than thinking of you as a company? How about shopping on Christmas Eve for the most sought-after, yet widely unavailable gift on the market? Both dating and shopping on the busiest day of the year require focus, persistence, a competitive edge and a will to win. The more special the prize, the harder you must work and the more avenues you must be willing to explore.

Ancient courtesans specialized in being special and exotic in order to gain the competitive edge. They took winning men seriously, and as a result they made sure that they were highly educated, academically, politically, artistically, sexually and socially to set them apart from the competition—all other women. They did not have formal educations or family money. But they made sure that one way or another they learned the art of love and the art of sex, which was not just about sexual acts. It was about seducing men from the inside out—from the top to the bottom—from his mind to all other extremities. They knew how to seduce a man's mind—and they knew that the rest of his body would follow.

They learned how to fence and they learned how to sing. They were musicians and poets and painters as well as great conversationalists that men could talk to about worldly events, in a way that they could not talk to their own wives who were not educated like the courtesans. Some of these women did not have beautiful faces or beautiful figures, in fact many of them were not beautiful at all—and those that had married men as lovers were often not as beautiful as the men's wives, but these courtesans attracted men like metal to a magnet because they took exquisite care of themselves—their bodies, their clothes, their grace, and most importantly, their minds. This made them valuable commodities, and the most educated and wise in allure among them, were the most valuable. When these women entered a room, their carriage and preening qualities made men stop and take notice, with awe and with respectful lust.

Some people daydream about fishing, but are afraid to leave the dock. Others have learned that the more times you go out and cast your net into the water, the better your chances of catching a fish.

—John Capozzi

To further illustrate the history of the Numbers Game, let's look at some contemporary women who have come from meager means, and built empires (and literally—corporations) based on their "best" selves as products. Cindy Crawford made her body WITH an ugly mole into a million dollar beauty trademark. Barbra Streisand made her face with a big nose famous, as she nourished her voice and her acting career to become the star of Oscar winning movies. Jennifer Lopez made a big behind, something that most women had previously spent lifetimes trying to loose, into a sexy body part that has become something clients ask plastic surgeons all over the country to duplicate on them. Lopez focused on what she was good at—her dancing, her particular beauty and her singing and acting—and of course, her love affairs and marriages. None of these women, without their makeup, their clothing and their money would win a beauty contest. But oh, how they know how to market themselves and get what they want!

Madonna has perhaps undergone more transformations than any public figure, simply because she's wanted so much and so many different things. She continues to change and grow, and nourish her image and her enormous allure. She came from little money, and suffered a loss in the death of her mother when Madonna was young. She learned to dance and to sing. She learned the music business—not just the music, but how to market her best self. When she first became a star, it was not because of a svelte body—although she has one now. She became a star because of her style, and she became a vixen because of her enchanting ways and attitudes. Her body, her face, her moves, her personality, her boyfriends, her family life—all morphed—because she deemed them to. She went from vamp to tramp to virgin to wife and mother, she's built a financial fortune, an artistic ouevre, a yoga body to be envied, two kids, movies, music, books and now a new religious life! Another enchantress is Cher, who came from meager means, with an imperfect face, but also with a drive, intelligence and a sarcastic wit that brought her a sexual aura and a presence. She learned to sing and dance and act. She went from a veritable joke on a variety TV show to an Oscar award winning actress, who's dated whomever she wanted from younger man to men her own age (whatever that is this year) to those who would be gay except for a relationship with her, because she set herself apart and continues to do so.

And then there is the big "O".

Oprah. She is one of the richest, self-made women in the world. She constantly strives to put forth her best show, her best body (we've all watched her yo-yo diet and try every exercise trend), her best magazine and her best public image. We buy Oprah because Oprah tells us, through every avenue possible, that she is at the top of her game. She gives us the idea that she is the best and we buy it. Yes, it's that simple. And ladies, I want to point out that ever since Oprah has turned into this thin, well dressed, bombshell, her viewers and sales have grown, as has the public demand for her. And remember, though Oprah is a drastic example, she is someone that has met with as many obstacles as anyone else. It is important to remember that even Oprah has failed. She has failed at dieting. She has had problems like everyone else—and more so. But every day, she puts her best inner and outer self forward.

Can you imagine if Oprah had let her failure get to her? We would have never even heard of her. But instead, she owns the world. What I'm getting at here is that you need to realize that failure is often a precursor and an ongoing part of success. Success is often perception and attitude. If you're having problems winning The Numbers Game, and you feel like you're low on fuel—change your attitude. It's a sure fire way to win this game.

> *There are only two kinds of people in the world: Those who think they can and those who think they can't. Both are right.*
> —Anonymous

Attitude

If you think you can, you can. And if you think you can't—you're right! Your biggest battle is in your own mind. Your mind can either cast doubt or enable you. If it's one or the other, why not choose the latter?

Positive thoughts produce positive results. Negative thoughts produce negative results. Attitude communicates your opinion of yourself, of other people, of business, and of life in general. Your thoughts become your reality. You become what you think about most.

Lance Armstrong. Being a good-looking man is not his only achievement. He has won the Tour-de-France six times, tying the world record. He's arguably the greatest cyclist of all time and certainly one of the world's best athletes. What has gotten him there? Maybe genetics, maybe a little luck, maybe enough corporate sponsorship for the best training facilities possible. Maybe.

However, he has DEFINITELY gotten there because of his attitude. Despite being diagnosed with Hodgkin's disease, he never lost sight of his goal. He maintained a great attitude and he persevered, and overcame cancer. He came back a champion.

> *Shoulda, coulda, and woulda won't get it done. In attacking adversity, only a positive attitude, alertness, and regrouping to basics can launch a comeback.*
> —Pat Riley, former L.A. Lakers Coach

ATTITUDE is absolutely essential as one of the main components of your corporation that is selling your dating self. If you have every other component and a bad attitude, you will lose sales and decrease your chances of finding the man of your dreams.

Now come back to The Numbers Game for one last point. Pretend that you own a men's cologne franchise. Would you expect that every single sexy man who walks into your store is going to buy a bottle of your scent? Would you take it personally if you approached a hot guy and asked, "Would you like to try our newest cologne?" and he said, "No, thank you, I'm just looking," and then proceeded to walk out of your store without purchasing? No, I really don't think you would because you've eliminated the unrealistic ideas like fate and romance. You're now a practical woman in business. You just gave him a simple sales pitch: some guys buy it, some guys don't. The idea is that the better your product, the better odds you have.

Dating is no different. Not every man is going to "get" you, just as not every man is going to buy your type of cologne. And I hope you can see now how ridiculous it seems to think they might! There will always be another customer, another potential sale, or another good-looking man. And you will always be evolving as a "product."

OK. So if dating is all about sales as a numbers game, how do you increase your odds of winning? Well, that is what the rest of this book is about. Each chapter is a piece of the dating puzzle. By the end of this book, you will have accumulated all the pieces and you will know the fundamental dynamics of dating, along with having realized a strategic plan for implementation. All that will be left for you to do is follow through.

Sales. Attitude. Follow-though. Repeat.

INTERESTING STATISTICS:

Our nation is teeming with 86 million adult singles.
According to the 2000 U.S. Census, there are mobs of divorced, widowed, never-married Americans eligible for the re-dating game.

What does this mean to you?

If you're 25 to 29, you have 9 million unattached peers.
If you're 35 to 44, you have 13 million unattached peers.
If you're 55 to 64, you have 2.3 million unattached peers.

In addition to those numbers:
Singles make up 42 percent of the workforce, 40 percent of homebuyers and 35 percent of voters.

Our culture remains marriage-centric. Almost 75 percent of us walk down the aisle by age 35, 95 percent by 65.

E-poll survey/Bridge Entertainment, Inc. All rights reserved.

4

Wanna Hear A Secret

◆

That Will Make You So Sexy You'll Attract The Most Wealthy And Successful Men? Come Closer...

> *It ain't what they call you, it's what you answer to.*
> —W.C. Fields

What's the number one thing that a man will find sexy? Okay ladies, I've told you to "think and date like a man," so you're probably thinking that the answer is either boobs, hips or lips. And yes, men are attracted to all of those things, but the number one quality that you must possess to attract a successful man is confidence. (That's C-O-N-F-I-D-E-N-C-E.) Coincidentally, confidence is also the key attribute that all professional salesmen must possess, in order to be successful. People do not buy products or services from a person who has no confidence in their products they represent. Remember, in the dating world, the product you represent is you! Within the dynamics of dating, if you're playing the Numbers Game, you are the salesman and men are your customers. It is up to you to sell the product with assurance and believability. If you lack confidence in your product—in yourself—it will show. Even if you say things that you believe make you sound confident, if you don't feel it, your nonverbal communication will give you away. In order to be successful with men, as in sales, you must have absolute confidence throughout the whole dating process. Know that you're going to 'close the deal.'

Think about it: why would he have confidence in you if you don't have confidence in yourself?

Physical beauty is ephemeral, but the self-confidence one builds from achieving difficult things and accomplishing goals is the most beautiful thing of all.

—Madonna

Where does confidence come from?

"Well, confidence comes naturally," you might say. "You either have it or you don't." Not true. In fact, confidence is simply what you get from doing things well, and realizing it. It's not a genetic lottery prize. Confidence comes with talent and accomplishment and skill, and the self-awareness to realize you have this gift. Other people will recognize your expertise and acknowledge it or compliment you on it. This is like water to a plant. Your confidence will build and grow, and create an inner glow as well as an outer draw.

To become good at something, the first step is to (have the confidence to) admit anything you don't know, in order to be able to decide to conquer it. If you pretend you know things you don't, you will be found out, eventually. False confidence smells like garbage. It's equivalent to a lie. It repels instead of attracts. Much better to say, "I don't know," or "I've never seen this. Will you show me how?" In fact, it's charming.

Take inventory of what you do and do not know, and then choose to educate yourself in areas you like or are lacking in—conversation, music, sex, dining—maybe you'll want to learn more about international politics. Perhaps it's dancing you want to perfect. Or you're invited to an art auction and don't know the first thing about them, so it's time to start learning. What if you're invited to a seven-course formal dinner, a horseshow—or even a high roller poker game! Whatever it is—and hopefully over time you will have many areas of expertise—indulge yourself in the nourishment of these arts. Because confidence is a characteristic that you obtain, the important thing is to begin progressively building it now, and then continue adding onto that foundation for life.

The more you know, the more confidence you'll have. Since many of these areas have lost their tutors to time, and charm schools are a thing of the past for the most part, you need to turn to books, classes and friends to teach you. (You may end up meeting a great guy with the same interests along the way.) Refuse to not know. Take care of yourself and your confidence will sprout up and grow. Your passion for what you love will be contagious, and sexy, and men will not be able to stay away from your spark or the flame it ignites.

> *Confidence—it comes from knowing what to do and how to do it.*
>
> —April Masini

Women with the most self-confidence are absolutely sure of who they are, what they want, and how to get it. And they do get it! The confident woman is a pink (and very cute) steamroller; she paves her own path. It doesn't matter what's going on around her (or who is around her). She focuses on the result she desires, and consistently takes the necessary actions to achieve it.

Passion
Your energy, enthusiasm and passion make all the difference when it comes to attracting men. If you want to build confidence and become more exciting to men, get passionate about your life—start really living. Do interesting things that add value to your life—and to other people's lives. Be an asset to your community, to your state and your country. Be an expert. There is no better way to be noticed by incredible men.

Men are attracted to passionate, exciting women with style. Yes, they're drawn to physical beauty, but physical beauty is less important than being a strong, dynamic woman whose eyes light up when she talks about what she loves. And I'm not talking about a big shoe sale here. (Most men are not going to want to talk about clothing any more than you want to talk about NASCAR racing.) I'm referring to real, meaningful, and valuable ideas and interests, whether it's a new business you're starting, your involvement in a sport, or your participation in a political initiative or campaign. (Of course, men will subconsciously think that your passion will transfer to other areas—and it will!)

IMPORTANT TO REMEMBER: The scariest part of any situation is taking the first step. If you can take the first step the second step will be much easier, and the others after that, even more so. It often takes more energy to put thoughts and energy into motion than taking the actual action itself. You get in your car of life with a clear map and all you have to do is start the engine. The rest is cruise control baby!

INTERESTING STATISTICS:

Most unique dating experiences
Following are the 5 most unique dating experiences that the respondents remember:
Among Women:
The date where I met my spouse (6%)
Romantic dinner/evening (6%)—which is significantly above Men (3%)
Beach date (5%)
Flying to a date (2%)
Blind date (2%)

Among Men:
The date where I met my spouse (5%)
Sex (4%)—significantly above Women (0%)
Beach date (3%)
Blind date (3%)
Romantic dinner/evening (3%)
Surprisingly, men cited falling in love (1.4%) significantly above the women (.2%) as the most unique date experience they can remember.
© E-Poll / Bridge Entertainment, Inc. All Rights Reserved.

5

Conquer Fear

> *The vast majority of people compare themselves unfavorably with others, dwelling on their own weaknesses and limitations as opposed to taking control of their lives and striving for what they want.*
> —Abraham Maslow, founding father of human psychology

You really are what you think. And sadly, most people sell themselves short and end up with far less than they are really capable or deserving. We human beings tend to be plagued with self-doubt, a lack of confidence, and fears of almost everything imaginable. Most of the time, our fears are unfounded and simply based on our insecurities—or our own feelings of inadequacy or things we simply don't understand and can't explain. This fear and its ancillary, anxiety, erode our confidence. If left unchecked, fear can completely destroy your confidence, and your dating life. The more fear you harbor, the more you will attract fearful men, and the more apt you (both) are to sabotage and destroy your relationships.

To begin to conquer fear, allow yourself to take control of your conscious mind and purposefully think of who you want to become, as opposed to who you aren't, and—this is the hard work—why you aren't where you'd like to be. While figuring out what is keeping you from your goal, (because this is a process and not a one day, or even one week long start to finish project), also focus on what you want, rather than what you're afraid you can't have. This process will begin a huge leap towards conquering fear.

"Yeah, easier said than done," you're probably thinking. Not really. Fear is a beast like any other. One to be confronted, tackled, wrestled to the ground and conquered.

> *It's not whether you get knocked down. It's whether you get up again.*
> —Vince Lombardi

Let's address five specific types of fear connected to dating.

1. Fear of Disapproval or Rejection—The method for conquering a fear of disapproval or rejection is to understand that you simply cannot please everyone—it's physically impossible. You cannot do it. Which means, you're not supposed to do it. You're not expected to do it—by anyone who's sane. (And if you're dating anyone who's insane, let's eliminate them right here and now.) You must not expect yourself to do the impossible. You must accept that fact that everyone has different motives, goals, tastes, likes, and dislikes. You will not be everyone's cup of tea, nor will everyone be yours. You will be rejected or disapproved of by some men. And you, too, will reject and disapprove of men, as well. You need to expect that it will happen. And while it can be painful and hurtful to realize you're not "good enough" for someone—yikes, think about what would happen if no one rejected anyone! You would date the wrong people, who didn't really love you, but didn't want to hurt your feelings, and waste your time—and their time! You would both be living lies and hurting each other in the long run. You would be spending your most precious commodity—time—with the wrong person! Doesn't that make rejection seem like a gift, now?

What matters is that you remain true to what you know to be important and right, and count on others to do the same. If you are certain about who you are and what you want, you will be able to put this fear aside because your opinion, and those of others, will be guideposts along the road to success. A rejection, like a flashing red light, will keep you from going down the wrong road.

I don't know the key to success, but I know the key to failure is trying to please everybody.

—Bill Cosby

---

2. Fear of Failure—The key to overcoming the fear of failing is to change your concept and definition of failure. True failure is lying: Lying to others is failure, and lying to your own self is the worst failure of all. Anything else is just an obstacle along the way. Embrace perseverance. Embrace the idea that this search for the right man is precious and when you find him, you will value the relationship because of all the hard work it took. Embrace everything you're learning along the way.

Diamonds are expensive because they are precious. They are not easy to find or cut. The same is true with oil. Treat your dating life with the same respect. Who said it was going to be easy? See the world and your dating life in terms of batting averages and practice shots—not perfection. Recognize that even the best of the best miss over 50% of the time, in fact the best home run hitters in professional baseball are the ones that strike out the most. Most successful home run hitters spend most of their baseball careers striking out. They are famous, however, for that handful of those out of the park wallops. Every time you step up to the plate and take a swing, you're getting one step closer to realizing success.

3. Fear of The Unknown—The things we don't know, can't understand, or can't explain, are what I refer to as, "fear of the unknown." For instance, when we were children, we feared darkness and the boogeyman. As an adult, we may fear people of different cultures and beliefs or situations that are new and different. There is a simple remedy for this kind of fear—knowledge. Knowledge brings a comforting familiarity to the unfamiliar, unheard-of, and obscure.

4. Fear of Change—Whether it is a new situation, like moving to a different state, a new challenge, like getting divorced, or a new job, many of us fear change. The antidote for this type of fear comes in the form of the confidence we gain from accomplishing goals, overcoming hardships, and meeting challenges…however small they may be. The first change is always the hardest, but when we see that the roof doesn't fall in, we will be able to remember it next time we face a change and do so with less fear and more grace.

> *You can't steal second base if you always keep one foot on first.*
>
> *—John Capozzi*

5. Fear of Success—Few address their fear of success because it can be hard to even believe it exists. Yet it is a very real and very prevalent fear for many of us. Often a fear of success comes from a deep seeded belief that we do not deserve success, so we subconsciously sabotage ourselves. We do this by creating drama, often. Breaking up with a boyfriend or husband or starting a fight when things are calm, are other ways we sabotage our success and happiness. If you find yourself doing this, try to figure out where the idea that you don't deserve something

came from. The more aware you are of the origins of this fear, the better chance you have of uncovering it, examining it, and conquering it.

Who better than Nelson Mandela to show us the light in—"Our Deepest Fear".

Our deepest fear is not that we are inadequate,
Our deepest fear is that we are powerful beyond measure.
It is our light, not our darkness that most frightens us.
We ask ourselves, who am I to
be brilliant, gorgeous, talented, and fabulous?
Actually who are you not to be?
You are a child of God.
Your playing small doesn't serve the world.
There is nothing enlightened about shrinking
so that other people won't feel insecure around you.
We were born to magnify the glory of God that is within us.
It's not just in some of us; it's in everyone.
And as we let our light shine,
we unconsciously give other people permission to do the same.
As we are liberated from our own fear,
our presence automatically liberates others.
—Nelson Mandela

Tackling fear can be tough, however there is no surer way to build confidence than to confront these types of difficulties—and defeat them!

6

First Impressions: Hit Them With Your Best Shot!

✦

Don't Pull Your Punches And Leave 'Em Reeling

> *You never get a second chance to make a first impression.*
> —Everyone's mother

First impressions. They are immediate, they are long lasting, and they are permanent. No matter how terrific you are, no matter how much your girlfriends, your parents and your dog all love you, no matter how absolutely amazing you can be once someone gets to know you, the reality is this: Your success with the people that you want to impress, including potential boyfriends, husbands and employers—will be based almost entirely upon someone else's perception of you within the first three to 17 seconds of your first encounter. Even if the perception is wrong, it is a fact that people sum up their interest in you almost instantaneously—and they believe their first opinions. An impression is a simple, primal response that is formed instinctively and takes a shockingly short amount of time to get. And once locked in, it is very difficult to change…in fact, most experts agree—impossible.

> *Remember, the first time you meet a man you have an opportunity that will never come again—the chance to make a good first impression!*
> —April Masini

The question is, will you—either positively or negatively—effect and influence that first judgment. Will it be you getting the date with the successful man you've

34

got your eye on, or will he be asking out the well-dressed woman with impeccable manners next to you (you know the one who's got half the brains and personality as you but somehow comes across as more together)? Will you accept the fact that looking the part is one giant leap toward actually being the part?

The way your potential date or lover judges you is crucial. If his first impression gives him the idea that you're his social equal, he'll think you're worthy of his attention. If it tells him you could be a bit better than he is, he'll admire you and want to know more. But if he perceives, during this initial encounter, that you have less class or social skills than he does, you won't be taken seriously—not for the job, not for a dinner date and certainly not for a life mate (that only happens in the movies). Which is not to say he wouldn't welcome a "roll in the hay"—but chances are good, that's all it will be.

While it may seem unjust that people make judgments based upon an initial impression of only a few seconds, the great part is that your image—and the judgments others make about you based upon it—is totally within your control! Now that you grasp the importance of your image, it's time to actually do something about it.

Look the Part: Getting your foot in the door
Physical appearance does not say everything about us, but it does say something about us, and it is the only part of us most people will experience in a brief encounter. Our exteriors are our instant messengers (IM's) to everyone around us. People will be automatically able to deduce some information about us. Why not try to put out your best information?

Studies show that the tallest, best-looking and most likeable people always beat out other candidates for the job. If you're going to think and date like a man, you'd better think of each first date like a first job interview. Consider the reality show, "The Bachelor." There are fifty women that make an initial impression on the first episode of each season. Note the most put together, attractive women in that first segment and then notice which of those women are still competing at the end of the show. I believe you'll find that those women who made the best first impression are the same women who go to the final ceremony.

Even if you prefer jeans and t-shirts in your leisure time, you wouldn't wear that outfit to a date with a successful man. You'd dress like you belong with him. It's that simple. Remember that old adage, "Dress for who you want to be, not who you are." It holds true in every aspect of your life—especially in love.

> *I celebrate myself, and sing myself, and what I assume you shall assume, for every atom belonging to me as good belongs to you.*
> —Walt Whitman (1819–1892)

In fact, why not take it one step further. Think about what you want your date's first impression of you to be. Instead of passable—why not knock his socks off? And continue to do so on each subsequent date (and every day you're with him, whether or not it's for the rest of your life). Imagine looking so stunning that he has a visceral and physical reaction? What if you are so beautifully dressed and groomed (No man is going to want to date a woman with Bert and Ernie-eyebrows. There is a multi billion-dollar beauty industry at your disposal to help people who are constantly striving to look good.), that he doesn't notice the details—only that the entire picture you've presented is eliciting a sexual and romantic reaction that is making him want you? What if your smile is so engaging and enchanting that you can see the attraction he feels for you in his eyes—and even if your smile was something you forced yourself to put on, because when you were sad as a child, your mother told you to force yourself to smile because it would make you feel better—it ignites your warmth and genuine allure?

The answer to these questions is simple. You'll have made an incredible first impression—and he'll want to know more.

How You Look—Take Your Own Inventory
What can you do to give yourself the advantage so that he is not only reeling with delight and awe from the vision of your beauty, but he can't take his eyes off of you? Start, by giving a lot of thought and preparation to what your look should be and how to make it happen. And please. Dress for who you want to be, and not (necessarily) who you are.

To do this, the first thing you'll need is a full-length mirror, and the next thing you'll need to do is to stand in front of it and be brutally honest with yourself. Few of us (at least without cosmetic surgery) have a perfect face and figure.

Makeup that enhances good features and lightly covers minor flaws can be your best friend; so assess and identify all that's good about your face. Are your lips a little too thin but you have wide-set, big blue (or brown or hazel) eyes? The perfect arch of a brow, the appropriate eye shadow and a great, lengthening mascara will draw attention to the windows of your soul (and away from your mouth). Do you think your eyes are too small for your face, but you have a great mouth with plump, well-shaped lips even Julia Roberts would kill for? The right makeup, skillfully applied, will make your eyes look bigger and the lipstick with an inviting, kiss-me-quick gloss will draw attention to a mouth he'll want to have…well, you get the picture. Always have clean hands, manicured nails and freshly shampooed hair with a simple style that frames your face attractively.

Not a clue how to do your makeup? Educate yourself in the art of makeup and grooming. Pay special attention to "Oh Make Me Over," the chapter on make-up and hygiene. Go for a consultation with a professional make up artist; or (if your budget doesn't allow that) get yourself down to your local better department where each cosmetics company has its own consultant right there at the counter to show you how to use its products—and it's free.

You never get a second chance to make a first impression.
—Anonymous

Still looking in your mirror, let your gaze travel down to evaluate your body. Figure faults can be corrected with diet, exercise and the right foundation garment. Victoria's Secret has not-so-secret fashions that can give even a 32-A some alluring cleavage. Once you've decided on a diet and exercise regimen (more about that in "There's No Body Like A Hot Body"—another chapter), there are lots of things you can do while you're waiting for the desired results.

Walk Like a Lady
Your mother wasn't wrong when she told you to sit up straight. Believe it or not, posture and grace are just as important in our modern age as they were in times past—at least, they are in that elegant world of class you want to enter. In fact, good posture is the first step towards developing grace, and makes clothes hang better and creates a younger, more sophisticated appearance.

ALWAYS sit up straight and stand up straight. Mothers in that elegant world you're aiming for give their daughter's horseback riding and ballet lessons—both excellent ways to develop good posture—in addition to being favorite activities of the rich and sometimes famous. But even if you didn't have those advantages growing up, it's not too late to adopt them now. You could still take riding or ballet lessons (it's also a way to meet the divorced or widowed dad of one of those upscale girls), but there are also other ways to develop the excellent posture that says you've got class, confidence and style. Another posture enhancing exercise that is everywhere these days is Pilates. It was created for the dance community and bi-weekly sessions will make you longer and leaner. The private sessions are quite expensive, but many gyms now offer mat classes that do not utilize the usual machines, and there are many good tapes available for you to benefit from Pilates exercise at home.

Good posture can be learned and maintaining it is just a habit. Posture is also a sign of self-confidence. More often than not, the lonely, shy introvert who has little energy or self-esteem has poor posture, which can also convey the message, "I am not interested in what you are saying," or "I don't care much about this encounter/meeting/date." That is not the impression you ever want to give, so you must have good posture at all times and on all occasions, whether sitting in or rising from a chair or getting in and out of a Mercedes—or on and off a horse.

Get into the habit of checking your posture every time you pass a mirror or window, and ask yourself: Do you look tired? Are your shoulders hunched or rounded? Does your stomach protrude? Are you slouching? If your answer is yes to any of these questions you definitely need to work on your posture—and until you do, you can forget about making a positive first impression. Write yourself little notes to "sit up straight" and "walk tall" and post them on your refrigerator, your bathroom mirror, your front door (so it's the last thing you see when you go out) and even in your car.

> *My theory is that if you look confident you can pull off anything—even if I have no clue what I'm doing.*
> *—Jessica Alba*

Your body language creates PRESENCE, which can mesmerize men. 'Presence' is the magical ingredient that can distract from practically any shortcoming because how you carry yourself, and how you appear, physically, are powerful tools to create a good first impression.

INTERESTING STATISTICS:

- You have a 1 in 8 chance that a first date will call you for a second date after 24 hours have passed.
- $201 is the average amount that men spend on dates per month
- 17% is the chance of liking a date set up by a friend
- 79 percent of men will take 15 minutes on a first date to make up their mind whether or not to see the person again.
*based on a survey of 3000 IJL clients

7

Don't Pink-Think

✦

Dumbing Down Is Just Dumb. Smart Is Sexy!

Stupidity in a woman is unfeminine.

—Nietzsche

Whoever popularized the air-headed ditzy girl trend didn't do womankind a favor. Was it Chrissy Snow from Three's Company? Mallory Keaton from Family Ties? Britney Spears from every interview she does? Growing up, most girls try to act ditzy and dumb around boys because we presume that boys like that. Unfortunately, many grown women still act this way around men. Perhaps they think that acting dumb makes them cuter, or perhaps they think that it makes a man feel smarter. Whatever the reason, they are indeed pretty stupid, if they think it's true.

NEWSFLASH: Men (especially accomplished and successful men), do not want to date a dumb woman, and if they do it's only with short-term goals in mind, if you know what I mean. Men definitely do not want to bring a stupid girl home to meet their mama; they do not want a woman who is incapable of holding an intelligent conversation at their side for an important corporate dinner any more than they want a woman that they have deemed dumb having their children!

A successful man wants an intelligent woman at his side because she is stimulating to him, and ultimately, she makes him look better to both his family and to his associates. Who we choose to be our partners in life largely reflects who we are and what we want in life. If he takes a smart woman to company parties and social gatherings, she will be able to converse with his colleagues and friends. If his girl is both beautiful and intelligent, his friends will surely be impressed. Moreover, though appearance often brings two people together, commonality and personality is what keeps them together (along with great sex).

A successful man can date a myriad of sexy and beautiful, attractive women with nice bodies. The woman who stands out from the rest and who keeps him coming back for more is the one who knows how to seduce and captivate his mind. This is the woman who will fascinate him. In reality, the only thing a guy likes about a stupid woman is the fact that she might be easier to get into bed. Period. And that's not the picture you want to paint of yourself if you want a keeper of a man.

If you don't know, look it up!
Now, if you didn't score a 1600 on your college boards, don't worry. You do not have to hold a degree from a fancy school to be intelligent, but you do have to be knowledgeable, aware, informed, interested and interesting. Ivy League schools do not make you smart, but becoming informed about the world around you (current events, politics, culture and cultures, history, trends, sports, etc.) does. Now, if at this moment, you don't have a clue about these topics, don't despair.

Did you ever ask your mom what a word meant, only to hear those dreaded words "Look it up in the dictionary"? Our moms weren't trying to be mean or unhelpful. They probably did know what the word meant, but they were trying to teach us a very valuable lesson—use the resources available to you to educate yourself. Like Samuel Johnson said, "Knowledge is of two kinds: we know a subject ourselves, or we know where we can find information upon it." Knowledge is power and power is an aphrodisiac.

Ready to start boosting your brain's power?

- Read the paper and watch the news daily.

- Always be reading a book on the New York Times Best Seller list—it's on that list for a reason. Even if it's not the best book, it'll be a good topic of conversation.

- Read the classics. You'll be surprised at how many times references from classic books are dropped at parties, on television shows and in newspaper articles.

- Subscribe to a free e-mail newsletter to a word-a-day or interesting fact-a-day.

- Learn a few quick one-liners that take people an extra second to process. Remember, Shakespeare said, "Brevity is the soul of wit."

- Learn another language and have knowledge of other cultures. Travel to more places than the spa with your girlfriends.

- Watch the History Channel and the Discover Channel (they make learning easy and fun). Biography and A&E work too.

- Follow politics—they do affect you. And yes, get involved.

- Always speak with proper grammar. Don't answer, "Doin' good," when a man asks, "How are you?"

- Ask questions…it not only shows you have a curious mind and an honest interest, but is also a great way to engage in a conversation.

- Listen more…

> *To be conscious that you are ignorant is a great step to knowledge.*
>
> —Benjamin Disraeli

The other side of the coin: The Roseanne Barr

On the other hand, while men do want to date an intelligent woman, they do not want to date a know-it-all, any more than you want to date an obnoxiously, overbearing man. There are few things less attractive than a loud, pushy woman that asserts her opinion as total, indisputable fact—even when she's wrong.

This is not to say men do not like women with their own points of views and opinions. They do. But, men need to feel as if they are the leader. For a woman with strong opinions, this requires discretion and grace. For those of us who are used to speaking without thinking, making sure that a man feels like the leader in conversation may require some discipline, too. Your opinion and thoughts are extremely important, but the dynamic overrules. He wants you to be intelligent and interested, because this makes him feel like he has caught a great prize in you, but he wants to feel like he caught you—and if you are the leader in the conversation, you will diminish his feelings of prowess. He may question that he is the one doing the catching. That is why it is important to let him lead.

Good conversation also requires you to ask questions and to respond with follow up questions. In order to do this successfully, you must have knowledge on the topic at hand and you must listen closely to what he is saying. True engagement is what keeps a conversation lively, just like a sport. But like a sport, there are foul shots that you must not take. For example, there is a difference between prying and interrogating and asking interesting questions, for instance:

Do ask: "What is your most treasured memory?" "If you could trade lives with anyone, who would it be?" "What do you think of the current President?" "What made you want to go into (insert appropriate field), finance, law, medicine, etc.," "If you were back in college now, knowing what you know today, would you study the same thing?" "Who is your favorite athlete?" "Do you think pro athletes are over paid?"

Do not ask: "How much money do you want to make?" "What kind of car do you drive?" "What are you doing this weekend?" "When are you going to call me?" "When am I going to see you again?" "Do you like this color nail polish?" "Do you want to have children?" "What type of wedding dresses do you like?"

> *The only thing worse than an articulate incompetent is an opinionated ignoramus!*
>
> —April Masini

Quiet interest on your part, is also alluring. Believe it or not, one of the easiest ways to appear more intelligent is to stop talking—and listen. You can't stick your foot in your mouth, unless your mouth is open, right? Ironically, some men also say that they find those same quiet listeners to be the best conversationalists…though, often, these women have barely said a word. You can still be part of a conversation by quietly showing an interest without saying a word.

Men like to be respected and admired. The woman who demonstrates an interest in his opinions and views is showing she respects and admires his intellect, his thought process, and his way of thinking. This makes him feel respected and valued—and she has successfully stroked his ego. This 'intelligent' lady leaves a man feeling very good, both, about him—and about her…Without a doubt, he'll want to see her again. And wanting a woman—you—is what you want to inspire in your man.

A few final notes:

Don't list (or name drop) all of your successes, degrees, or status and ego related accomplishments into the conversation. You are on a date, not a job interview. If he wants to know about you, he'll ask. Besides, let him think he found these things out by his own cunning—not because you blabbed your resume. Equally, it is best to encourage a man to talk about himself and his accomplishments on the first few dates. As I mentioned before, one of the best ways to get a successful man interested in you, is to show great interest in him—specifically his opinions, his thoughts, and his intellect. You will also be able to figure out if this man is someone you want or not as you learn more about him without investing your own information and privacy. This overall dynamic creates enchantment and allure.

A truly smart (and charming) woman not only knows how to ask good questions, and be a good listener, she also knows how to flatter a man while keeping the conversation going with lines like: "That is fascinating, I never thought of it that way," or "Wow, that's really interesting—tell me more about that."

Beauty fades, dumb is forever!

—Judge Judy Sheindlin

Now, I do not want to imply that men aren't interested in accomplished women, or that they will not be interested in your accomplishments—they are—but when it comes to conversation, you can never go wrong by centering the focus on every man's favorite topic—him. There will be plenty of time for him to discover all the wonderful things you have done, once he realizes how much he wants you and wants to know about you. And the best way to get him interested in learning about you is to keep him talking about him.

Finally, just to be clear, there is a difference between knowledgeable, informed and opinionated women, versus argumentative, dogmatic and stubbornly hard-headed women. Any woman who insists upon having the last word in a social situation is not demonstrating signs of intelligence. In fact, she is socially ignorant. Not an attractive quality. Should you ever feel the urge to "have the last word," make sure it's when you're breaking up with the guy because if you're not—he will.

INTERESTING STATISTICS:

60% of households where the income earned was $50,000 or more and 56% of college graduates think that people have a better or equal chance of meeting someone that they like, online than at a single's bar.

This compares with 50% of households earning $25,000–$50,000 income and less than $25,000 households and 54% of those with some college and 48% of those with high school or less.

To break it down even further, among other subgroups, 55% of men and 50% of women think that people have a better or equal chance of meeting someone they like online than at a single's bar. This is also true among 53% of those aged 18–34 years, 57% of 35–54 year olds and 46% of those aged 55 years or more, including 55% of those who are currently married and 51% of those who are currently single, and 51% of residents in the Northeast, 52% Midwest, 53% South and 53% West.

Section II:
The Ladies' Locker Room

Now that you know how a man thinks and dates, and that the best way to seduce a man is to seduce him from the mind down, I'll tell you how to prepare yourself in ways that only women can do. Traditionally, the arts of fashion, grooming, etiquette and poise, as well as sex, were passed on from family member to family member, usually from a mother, an aunt or a sister to a daughter, niece or younger sister. If your mother gave you a cursory talk about the birds and the bees, and bought you a book about intercourse to reference if you had any questions, but she never told you about romance, or what makes a man want to love you, or how to kiss a boy good night—let alone if you should kiss him good night—if that was all you got, and it's no longer enough (not that it ever was enough)—you're not alone. If your mother bought you your first box of tampons, and showed you how to use them, but never taught you to pluck your eyebrows into a perfect arch that complements your face, or how choose the right shaped eyeglasses frames for your particular shaped face, you're not alone.

Let's get away from the body as a machine and get back to the body as a shrine. Here in the ladies' locker room, I'll show you the power you have that your mother didn't show or tell you. I know what it's like to be "out there," and I also know what it's like to get the most successful man in the room—and even to marry him. You can create looks that startle and allure him, by simply knowing what to wear on what occasion, and then putting your own style to work. Make up is an adornment that women in all cultures use to lure men to them. Fragrance is also an enticement that you can use to fascinate him. Allow him to be awed by your figure and the smoothness of your skin. Don't ignore all the power that you have at your fingertips. Your body is a gift—not just for health but also for pleasure. And while he will get friendship from the other guys, sport from pros at the gym, competition and financial gain from work, family from his mother's at Thanksgiving, the place he will turn for feminine companionship, a feminine point of view, and female pleasure must be you—and only you.

Female sexuality and sensuality has always included fashion, makeup, grooming, and sexual preparatory rituals in all cultures—it is only in recent decades that (mostly American) women have been told that their lives are utilitarian at most, and pleasurable as an afterthought—something to make time for, if any is left over. Even childbearing, one of the most private and sacred female functions has taken on a scientific and medical tone rather than one of original spirituality, religion and sensuality. Many women now decide when to have children based on how their work schedules mesh together with their husbands, ignoring their own bodies and their own inner sources. Women have tremendous power from the universe, but they forget or they ignore it. Think about your menstrual cycle, and notice how it is allied with the lunar calendar. Notice carefully how your sexual drive ebbs and peaks with your cycle, how your moods change regularly during the month, how your appetite changes—all on a cycle. It is easy in all the hustle bustle and confusion of gender role-playing to lose track of your instincts that are there to guide you.

I want you to go back to your instincts and celebrate your femininity with clothing, make up and grooming rituals. Wear lingerie that makes you feel sensual. Wear shoes that make you walk like you want more than just to get to your meeting—they make you want feel sexual at the same time. Wear earrings that dangle and touch the side of your neck to remind you that your skin feels. Take care of your body—not just with shampoo and soap and shaving your legs (although all that is important)—but with massage and fragrance and exfoliant on a loofah sponge. Notice what a french manicure does to the way you use your hands or what a bikini wax does to the way you move in a dress.

Allow your body to be the ultimate gift to a man—not just for his pleasure, but for him to see yours, as well. His greatest goal is to make you feel feminine and sexual. No man wants a woman to be competing with him—unless of course she's willing to lose every time. The more feminine you feel and appear, the more masculine he will feel, and that's what it's all about. The differences.

Knowing this, you can use what you have in your body, your height, your gait, your glance, your poise and your etiquette to entice, allure and make him feel manly.

Were we living in another time, you might be labeled a witch if you confessed that you were enticing a man. In fact, some people—most of them men—are so befuddled by a woman's powers that they call them black magic (Black Magic Woman is a great example of how a man sings that he's had a spell put over him by a woman.), and make them the subject of songs, books, movies (Practical Magic, Witches of Eastwick, etc.) and all kinds of art. Some people even blame feminine wiles for their downfall—and they wouldn't always be wrong. Femininity is that strong. When you read and use all the tools in this section of the book, you will be closer than ever to being the legendary, mythical and rare woman who can turn powerful men to putty and moguls to mice. You will be called on for advice, and longed for after your advice is dispensed.

8

Mistress Manners!

Proper etiquette is essential to be a world-class date and to date first class!

—April Masini

No man wants to date a slob, and a man who is successful and wealthy will expect you to have proper etiquette. In fact the better your manners, the more he will feel as if he is in the company of royalty—and that will make him feel like he has a great prize in you. Good manners are just as much an attribute as great legs or a beautiful face. Chances are your man will want to take you places where everyone else will already know their Ps & Q's. You don't want to lose favor with him or his colleagues or family because you don't know which fork is which. And if you think they don't notice these things, you're wrong. They do. Manners make a difference.

Proper etiquette will:
• Add polish and presence and outclass the competition
• Increase your power, confidence, and credibility
• Ensure that your image makes a positive and bold statement
• Strengthen your ability to persuade and inspire others as they view you in a more positive light

Rudeness is the weak man's imitation of strength.
—Eric Hoffer

As a woman, there are certain codes of chivalry that your date will already know and practice, and you should know what he knows so you don't create an awkward situation by grabbing for the door split seconds before he does. Here's how a gentleman behaves:

Codes of chivalry
A gentleman always...
• Walks ahead of a lady coming downstairs to prevent her from slipping and falling
• Walks on the curb side of a sidewalk
• Rises when a lady enters or leaves a room
• Follows a lady to a table, pulls out her chair and steadies it as she sits
• Allows the lady to walk ahead of him into the row of a movie theater or at a sports event
• Unlocks the passenger door from the outside, helps the lady into the car, then closes her door
• Gets out first on arrival, calmly walks to her side, and helps the lady out (running to her side as if you're sprinting in a marathon is definitely not cool)
• Helps a lady into a car—even if she is the driver

A lady always allows and expects all of the above. Men love being the man, and if you play the part of the lady, it will make him feel more like a prince. And what's wrong with that?

Casual greetings
• A nod and a smile are all that are necessary when casual acquaintances pass by.
• Saying "hi" is also sufficient—and remember, it's a great way to make initial contact with men.
• If someone is too far away to speak to without shouting, simply smile and wave—never look like you're trying too hard.

The rules to introductions
Introductions are required when two strangers meet in the company of a mutual friend. If you are the mutual friend, you must introduce the two people who do not know each other. Not to do so is inexcusably rude. When you do introduce two people, follow these basic rules:

• A man is always introduced to a woman.
• A young person is always introduced to an older person.
• A less important person is always introduced to a more important person.
• Except for members of your family, no woman is ever presented to a man unless he is: the head of a country, a member of a royal family, a church official, or an older man in high position, such as a governor. In addition to the rule that younger people do not address significantly older people by their first name

(unless asked), there are others for whom first names may not be used except by specific request as well.
• A superior in one's business, unless it is obviously the office custom
• A business client or customer, until requested to do so
• A person of higher rank (a governor, a diplomat, a senator, for example)
• Professional persons offering you their services, such as doctors and lawyers, who are not personal friends

> *Confidence comes from knowing what to do and how to do it.*
> —April Masini

How to shake hands
His handshake is brief, with firmness and warmth in the clasp, accompanied by his looking directly into your eyes. Don't try to match his grip. He wants to feel your warmth, and your femininity, but not the entire effect of your gym membership.

Goodbyes
Okay, now that you've mastered hellos, let's move onto the goodbyes. The most cordial way to extricate yourself from a conversation is to say, "Mr. Hottie, I'm so glad to have had this chance to speak with you, but I've got to go or I'll be late for my next appointment." If you are in a group, and are ready to leave, wait for a pause and then say, "Goodbye. I hope I'll see you again soon," or simply, "I'm glad to have met you." When leaving a group of strangers—whether you have been introduced or not—nod and smile good-bye.

Ladies first
In most circumstances, in-doors and out, when a couple walks together, the woman precedes the man, through a door, a narrow passageway, on the escalator, etc., except:
•If you two are walking over rough ground (e.g. a construction site), the man goes first and offers his hand if you need assistance.
• When he opens the car door, you get in first.
• If you're going down a steep ramp or a slippery stairway, you go first.
• When stepping onto a boat or a bus, he helps you on first.

Walking together
A man generally walks on the street or on the curbside of a woman to protect her from cars splashing or spraying dust or dirt. If he prefers to ignore the curbside tradition entirely, he will walk on the woman's left. When walking or sitting with a man and a woman, you should be seated so that you can look directly into his eyes while talking. Avoid sandwiching him between you and the other woman. Resist the urge to sandwich yourself between them (best left to his private fantasies.)

> *Politeness and consideration for others is like investing pennies and getting dollars back.*
> —Thomas Sowell

Elevator etiquette
The man or woman nearest the door enters first and holds the "door open" button for those following, and the person nearest the door steps off first when exiting.

Smack, crackle, pop
Chewing gum in itself is one thing, if done discreetly. Chewing your gum like a cow gnawing its cud or blowing bubbles is quite another. Keep it quiet. Keep the gum in your mouth.

Smoking in public places
Smoking has become a socially unacceptable habit. But if you still persist, the law in most states now governs exactly where you can and cannot smoke. I suggest you don't do it at all, as it will significantly decrease your chances of finding dates. If that's not incentive to quit, I don't know what is.

PDA'S (public displays of affection)
Let's talk about PDAs. Everyone's got an opinion on them, but the truth is, there are some basic rules to follow. Holding hands, affectionate greetings accompanied by a kiss on the cheek, or quick hugs are perfectly acceptable in public. Mauling your lover is not. Get a room, ladies (exhibitionists exempt)!

Consideration for those who serve
It is inexcusable and low class to be inconsiderate of the professionals who serve you in bars, in restaurants, in shops, or elsewhere in public. This sort of arrogance and discourtesy is a definite indicator of insecurity, and totally unattractive.

> A person who is nice to you, but not nice to the waiter, is not a nice person.
>
> —David Barry

Visiting
Never be an unexpected visitor. And I mean never! Catching him off-guard is invasive.

Illness
Whether you've been dating six days or six months, it is the height of thoughtlessness for a man, with a cold or another infectious illness, to be in the company of a lady and pass your illness on to her. If you desire companionship when ill, use the telephone. If she's into you, she'll probably offer to bring soup or medicine by, but let the choice be hers.

Table manners matter
The fact is budding executives and professionals have been passed over for promotions because their table manners were unpolished, even though their job performance was exemplary. Now if your boss is going to pass on you because you eat with your hands, how on earth do you expect a man you want to date to want to watch you slurp soup and cut your dinner roll with a knife? Proper etiquette is just that important!

Posture at mealtime
Your posture at the table should be straight, but not stiff, leaning slightly against the back of the chair. Slouching or slumping at the table is unattractive and signals disrespect for your dining companion.

When you are not eating your hands should lie in your lap when you are not using them. This will automatically prevent you from fussing with silverware, playing with breadcrumbs, or drawing on a tablecloth and so forth. Fidgeting is a sign that you are not focused on him.

• If you can't resist the temptation to fidget, you may rest your hands and wrists—but not your entire forearm—on the table.
• Elbows are never on the table when one is eating.
• Tipping on one's chair is unforgivable.

The napkin
Ordinarily, as soon as you are seated put your napkin on your lap, however at a formal dinner, wait for your hostess to put hers on her lap first.
• Do not give a violent shake to your napkin in an effort to open it.
• Never tuck your napkin into your collar, belt, or between the buttons of your blouse.
• Do not use the napkin to wipe your mouth as if it were a washcloth.

When the meal is finished, or if you leave the table during the meal, put the napkin on the left side of your place setting. If the plate has been removed, rest your napkin at the center where your plate used to be. Lay the napkin in loose folds and do not refold or crumple it. When you feel a sneeze or a cough coming on, cover your mouth and your nose with your handkerchief, or if you do not have one, or time to get it out, use your napkin. Never use your napkin to blow your nose. If you are caught without a handkerchief or a tissue, excuse yourself and head for the nearest bathroom.

Start Eating
At a table of two, four, or six people, you wait to start eating until all have been served. When there is a clear host or hostess, wait until she picks up her utensil, the others should follow suit. If the group is very large, it is not necessary to wait until all have been served.

The Silver—From the Outside In
This can be a telltale sign of one's "class," so pay close attention! You always start with the implement of each type that is farthest from the plate. So if salad is served as a first course, grab the fork that is farthest from your plate—that is the salad fork. After finishing the main course, place the knife and fork beside each other on the dinner plate diagonally from the upper left to lower right. The desert spoon or fork is placed in the same position.

Fork and Knife
You can never go wrong with the American custom of "zigzag" eating (changing the fork from left to right hand after cutting meat). The simpler European method is leaving the fork in your left hand after you have cut your meat, and eating the meat from your fork while it is still in the left hand.

"Pushers"
A piece of bread crust is the best pusher. It is held in the left hand in the same position as when cutting with the right hand, and the tip of the blade is to guide and push the food onto the fork. If properly used, the knife is also correct.

Tooth-pickers
Toothpicks should not be used at the table, and you should not pick at food in your teeth with your finger. Excuse yourself and go to the bathroom to remove it, or wait until the end of the meal.

Pasta
When faced with a romantic Italian restaurant and a plate of spaghetti bolognese, do not cut your spaghetti and please, don't slurp it strand by strand. Likewise, don't shove a forkful into your mouth. Instead, use your big spoon in your left hand, and your fork in your right hand to gently twirl small forkfuls on the spoon, and neatly deposit them in your mouth. This is a polite and efficient way to keep the romance in the meal and the spaghetti in your mouth.

INTERESTING STATISTICS:

What makes an ideal first date? In one study, respondents were asked to describe their ideal first date with someone and below are the top 5 responses cited:

Among Women:
Going to lunch or dinner (50%)—significantly above men (42%)
Meet for coffee (13%)
Going to a movie (12%)
Going to an event (11%)
Going to the beach/park (8%)

Among Men:
Going to lunch or dinner (42%)
Going to a movie (16%)—significantly above women (12%)
Going to an event (12%)
Meet for coffee (11%)
Going to the beach/park (7%)

Single respondents are more likely to want to meet for coffee (15%) and go to the beach/park (10%) than the married ones (8% and 6%).

E-poll/Bridge Entertainment, Inc. All rights reserved.

9

Get A Good Hair-Fare

> *Life is an endless struggle full of frustrations and challenges, but eventually you find a hair stylist you like.*
> —Author Unknown

While sometimes it seems like men are just staring at your chest, (and sometimes they are!) the truth is that your face is the first thing they notice, and hair is the frame on the face. Socially, your hair is a cue that tells men about who you are. Power bobs and a sleek ponytail telegraph a message to the world that you're business-like, efficient, and that you have work to do—great for a job interview, but not for dating. Long locks tell the world that you're a sensual woman. You care about having hair that looks and feels good. You take care of your hair because sensuality, and looking sexy is important to you. The message you're telegraphing is that you'll take care of him in "that way" too. Sensuality and sexiness are important to you in more areas than just hair. Bottom line: you want your dating-self to have the kind of hair that makes him want to look at you again.

Men love women's hair, and they love it long, so I completely recommend a long hairstyle, but there are different ways to have long hair. You can have butt length hair, but you can also have shoulder length hair or below—the-shoulder length hair—all of which give you the look of having long hair. When making a decision on what works best for your dating-self, start with the big picture by looking at your body shape first, then look at your face shape.

Body Shape
The hair on your head affects your entire look, so if you are petite, hair down to your butt is going to make you look like Cousin It. If you are in your 20s you may not want a blown dry, "finished" look that is more mature than your years. And if you're (confessing to) 40, be careful that your hair doesn't look like it belongs on a teenager and that you're desperate to hold on to the past instead of enjoying all your assets (and hopefully his, too!) in the present. You want men to be comfortable with your hair, and that means you have to be comfortable with it too, not desperate.

Face Shape
Consider your face shape, your hair texture, and whether you have straight, curly, kinky or wavy hair before you pick a cut.

Your best asset: A super great haircut
A great haircut is like good health. You don't notice it until you don't have it. Nothing is more of a turn off than split ends, a grown out hair cut, etc. It just looks like you're not maintaining your best self. So keep up your hair. Even long hair needs to be trimmed regularly to keep it thick and clean lined. If your budget is limited, find a salon like Vidal Sassoon, which teaches future hairdressers, and needs models to teach on. You will wind up with a free haircut that is probably great.

Color hue tint shade
One of the most important aspects of your hair is color. There are several colors on your body that affect your hair color and vice verse. Besides your eyes and the clothing colors, there's your skin tone. Your skin has pink, green, blue or brown undertones which are important to consider when you determine what color hair is most flattering, as are your brow color, your freckles and any beauty marks. If you have green undertones, a brown hair color will be more flattering. Pink undertones are great for blonde hair.

If your skin is olive, you are best suited to dark hair. However, if you have dark skin tone, and are aching to try being a blonde, then opt for some highlights, which are specific sections of lightened hair, instead of going full on blonde. And don't lighten them too much, at first, so you don't loose touch with your organic look. If you like the look after your first salon appointment, make the next appointment with the goal being to have lighter highlights, and maybe more of them, too.

> *Gray hair is a sign of age. Not wisdom.*
>
> —Greek Proverb

Highlights
One simple way to graduate color changes and give your hair a beautiful, healthy looking glow in one quick trip to the salon is with highlights. Highlights are applied by the colorist, who picks strands of hair, then separates them from the

rest of your head, and brushes a lighter color dye on the separate strands. In order to make sure the dye doesn't touch the rest of your head, the highlighted strands are wrapped in tin foil, which is allowed to rest on your head while the color "sets." The result when the color sets is a more subtle color change. You can have your hair highlighted or you can have your hair colored, and also highlighted, so you're actually applying two different colors to your hair at once—your "base" coat, and the lighter highlight colors.

Lowlights
Lowlights are another creative choice to give your hair flair. If you're blonde and you want to see how you'll look a little darker, lowlights are dark colored highlights that can graduate your blonde to a dirtier blonde. You can do lowlights for one month, and then the next month, you can do a little more, and then gradually go for a browner look, or keep a dirty blonde look. This is a great way to go from a platinum, or very, very blonde, to an earthier blonde look.

How often should you color your hair?
Roots are ugly and sloppy. Don't let them show. The normal amount of time between coloring appointments is four to eight weeks. If you color your own hair, go to a beauty supply store, and ask for help choosing the correct products and color. The sales clerks are often very knowledgeable, and can help you choose the correct color and make sure you have rubber gloves, skin color remover and any other necessary gear. Some colors "set" darker than the sample in the store and a knowledgeable salesperson will steer you towards what is right for you.

Don't get brow beaten…
If you color your hair, make sure your brows are the same color, or close to it. If your brows are a noticeably different color than your new hair color, you can opt to color your brows, too. Or lighten them!

You can even have your eyelashes tinted—but keep in mind that the FDA has longstanding warnings against any use of permanent eyelash dyes and tints. It is not illegal, but be aware that if you do opt for this procedure, be extremely careful in choosing your licensed, professional aesthetician.

Farewell funky colors
Before you try a pink streak or blue tips just for fun, remember—Kelly Osborne gets away with pink hair because she's British, she's rich, she's 21 (if that) and her

father is a recovering heroin addict. Leave the crazy colors for Halloween or Hollywood rock royalty. Just because you broke up with your boyfriend or are newly divorced does not mean you should "live a little" by coloring your hair green. Not even for fun. Express yourself in your journal. Not your strands.

Factoid: The lifespan of a human hair is 3 to 7 years, on average.

Got gear?

Okay, you're home. You have a great new cut. You have new color. You have a bag full of product. You look like a million bucks. Now it's time to face a woman's greatest fear. The fear that far outweighs spiders, the dark and rats: THE SHOWER after a salon appointment!! What will happen to your great new style if you wash it and are left to make it look like it did the day you left the salon? How many days can you go without washing it so you don't have to face the dreaded "reconstruction?" Relax. Leave the horror to the horror movies. There is no reason you can't get your hair to look just as good tomorrow, as it looks today. You just need the right gear.

* A good hair dryer that powers up to at least 1200 watts and has at least three temperature settings. Also, make sure it isn't too heavy, so you don't pull a muscle drying your hair. Make sure to clean out the screen area in the back of the dryer every month. Dust and particles get caught in there, and will slow down drying time.

* A diffuser is an attachment that will spread the air out, when you're drying it—especially handy for curly or wavy hair, when you want to keep the curls or waves. Intense streams of heat will straighten hair, so if you want some curl, or want to protect your curl, pick up a diffuser to attach to your dryer.

* Brushes are an easy way to make your hair look great by using the correct ones. Paddle brushes are wonderful for long, straight hair. They straighten as they brush. If you don't want your hair straight, don't use a paddle brush. A vented brush with spaces between bristles is great for blow drying because the spaces allow the dryer air to circulate through your strands while you style, speeding styling. A brush with a hollow, metal core, essentially functions as curlers as you dry, transferring and holding the heat against the hair instead of it just blow

through your locks. Brushes with natural boar hair bristles are great for a finishing look.

"Hair style is the final tip-off whether or not a woman really knows herself."

—Givenchy, Vogue Magazine

Hair that's everywhere—else

Unless you're on the television show Survivor, and you have a realistic shot at a million dollars at the end of three months, get rid of the hair. Even if you are on Survivor—in fact, especially if you're on Survivor—find a way to get rid of the hair! What good is surviving if your legs look like a gorilla's legs? Men like women to have smooth, silky, hairless skin, and women have been getting rid of hair for men throughout the ages. In fact hair removal is thousands of years old, and archeologists have evidence of men shaving hair off their faces as far back as 20,000 years ago. Sumerians used tweezers; Egyptians took their bronze razors to their tombs with them, and beeswax was also in evidence as a hair removal tool even back then. Evidence of depilatories date as far back as 4000 to 3000 B.C. Evidence exists in ancient India of chest and pubic hair being shaved. Surprisingly, not a lot has changed in the temporary hair removal arena except for some of the ingredients. Hair removal as beauty is history that we want to repeat.

Temporary hair removal methods: Any kind of hair removal that lasts for fewer than three months.

1. Shaving is the obvious and easy choice. Treat shaving the same way you do brushing your teeth. Give your legs the same care you do your pearly whites. Keep your legs smooth the same way you keep your teeth clean.

2. Depilatories are creams that you can purchase in a beauty supply store or drug store that you apply to your body, in your own home. Depilatories contain chemicals that remove hair by chemically burning it. Therefore, you may smell an icky sulfur odor after using them. It will go away. It is important not to leave the depilatory on your skin for any longer than the directions on the package instruct in order to prevent burning your skin. The best reason to use depilatories is that you don't need to get an appointment in a salon to get a clean hair removal. They're inexpensive and easy and quick. Even if it's not your regular method of hair removal, consider it as a temporary measure if you're in a pinch.

Depilatory tricks:
* Before applying the depilatory, wet the area of skin and hair that you are going to treat, with warm water.
* When you're ready to remove the depilatory and dead hair from your body, don't spray water directly on skin to wash it all away. It's too harsh. Instead, use a warm washcloth to gently wipe the depilatory and dead hair away. This is easier on skin than a harsh stream of water pressure that may be too intense for your skin.
*Never use depilatories around your eyes, vaginal area, or any open or healing cut or scrape. Or anywhere else you wouldn't put a chemical.

3. Bikini waxing is the removal of hair along the "bikini line," which means there should be no hair left to see when you put on your bikini bottom.

Does it hurt?
Some women would rather have childbirth without anesthesia than have a bikini wax. Yes, it hurts. But it's not terrible for most people and it looks great. Besides, you do get used to it, and there are tips, below, for reducing the pain. A waxed bikini line looks a million times better than shaving. And the waxing technician can get the hair from nooks and crannies that you can't reach when you're shaving, or can't see when you're applying depilatory.

"The pain passes, but the beauty remains."

—Auguste Renoir

Is it embarrassing?
What's really embarrassing is having hair where you don't want it in a social or sexual situation. Men don't want too much hair down there, and once you realize that this is business—and trust me, your waxing technician makes her living because so many women pay her for her valuable service—you'll lose any and all embarrassment. Besides, if the only reason you may be embarrassed is if you've never done it before, so here's what happens: After you make an appointment (on the telephone tell the appointment person that you want a full leg, and/or a half leg—upper or lower, and/or a bikini wax) and show up at the salon, your waxing technician will most likely be a woman who will ask you to lie on a table in a private area or room, either in your underpants, or in a pair of paper panties your waxing technician will give you so you don't get wax on your own lingerie, or else

you'll be buck naked from the waist down. (Lying naked from the waist down, in a room with someone you don't know, who didn't go to medical school, and hasn't bought you a drink, is something you will have to get over.)

Aside from being naked, you're hairy. Don't apologize for the hair. And don't shave to try and make a good impression on a stranger by not having much hair. The biggest mistake you can make before going to a waxing technician, is shaving. Let the hair grow, and your aesthetician will have an easier time doing a good job waxing you, and you will have better results. If you happen to be hairy, don't worry about it. It's not illegal.

Your waxing technician will use what looks like a tongue depressor (remember those trips to the pediatrician?) to dip into a pot of melted wax, and she will spread the wax on your bikini area, then lay down strips of cloth and press down so that the cloth adheres to the wax, which has adhered to the hair on your body. It will feel somewhere between warm and hot. Tell her if it's too hot. The waxing technician will apply cloth strips to the wax, which she will pull off, removing the strips, the hardened wax attached to the strips, and the hair attached to the wax.

FACTOID: Hair is the fastest growing tissue in your body.

This hurts. But it's quick. And it's not as bad as going to the dentist, but if you've never had it done before, your skin will probably be sensitive. Your waxing technician should apply some cooling antiseptic like witch hazel, or some other soothing ointment afterwards. You may have a red rash for up to 24 hours, especially if you normally have sensitive skin. So don't have a bikini wax the same day or night that you will be in a bikini or showing off your body. Give yourself 48 hours so your skin can calm down.

How long does it take?
The entire process takes about fifteen minutes depending on how much hair you have. The more often you go, over the years, the shorter amount of time you'll have to spend to get good results. Your waxing technician may just do the front of your body. More thorough waxing technicians will do the sides of your legs, and have you flip over on your stomach so they can do the buttocks and backs of the thigh. The cost ranges between $45 and $75. Leave a 20% tip if you're happy.

The more often you get waxed, the less sensitive your skin will be and the thinner your hair will grow back. And the more often you get waxed, the more likely your hair will begin to die at the root, and diminish, making subsequent waxing less painful, quicker, and not as necessary. This hair loss won't happen overnight, in fact, if it does happen, it happens over a period of years.

Please put in a quote box: Ya know what, I think I'm gonna go to my room and read Cosmo, maybe there's something helpful in there. Know what, at least maybe I can learn how to do an at home bikini wax with leftover Christmas candles.
—Monica on NBC's TV show, Friends

Three different kinds of bikini waxes
*A Traditional Bikini Wax—removes the hair everywhere except where your bikini sits.
*A Brazilian Wax—A Brazilian bikini wax leaves nothing but a "landing strip" of hair, about two to three fingers wide, usually in the shape of an upside down triangle, on your labia. No hair is removed from your labia. Hair is removed from your buttocks. This wax is named for the beautiful Brazilians who wear the G-strings and thongs on the beach.
Sometimes the Brazilian wax is mistaken for the bare all wax where everything is taken off but your bare skin. The hair on your lips, the hair between your legs, and even the hair in and around your anus is gone, gone, gone. I know, I know. Thinking about the removal process is so bizarre, but it is truly a great experience to have nothing there but you.
*A Playboy Wax—does remove hair from the labia, the buttocks and buttock area including around the anus. All that is left of your hair down there is a very thin strip that resembles the waxes that the Playboy magazine centerfolds have.

Don't try this at home! The best way to find someone to perform these waxing treatments is through personal referrals or a reputable salon. This is not a process you want to leave to amateurs or bargain shop for.

Hazards of waxing:

* Ingrown hairs—prevent them by using an exfoliant scrub and a loofah sponge to clean and brush away dead skin and hairs that promote ingrown hairs, but only after 48 hours post waxing. After you have your legs waxed, don't forget to use a loofah sponge to exfoliate dead skin from the back of your legs, a traditional problem area.

How long does it last?

Three weeks in the summer, four in the winter, depending on how hairy you are.

Permanent hair reduction:

1. Laser treatment. This is the newest method of hair removal that you cannot do yourself. Approved for hair removal by the FDA in 1995, laser hair removal treatments—yes—plural: treatments—it takes more than one visit—removes hair with a laser beam that destroys the root and the shaft of the hair. Lasers use heat to damage dark target matter. This is one reason that laser hair removal is not good for African American skin. The laser can change the pigment of the skin while removing the hair, leaving a discolored area right where you want no attention at all! It is also why people with grey, blonde or red hair are not ideal candidates. Neither are people with olive or dark skin. The best candidates are people with light skin and dark hair.

Best place to get laser hair removal treatment is from a physician. A dermatologist or plastic surgeon is best. Treatments are scheduled at four to six week intervals, and how many you need has to do with the treatment and your hair. You will have to wear protective goggles during the treatments.

Laser removal does not work for everyone, so be prepared. Set up a consult appointment with your doctor to discuss before you commit. You can also set up an appointment for a "patch test," so you can see what the laser feels like, and what your re-growth rate is—if any. Don't sign up for treatment until after you wait a while to see if your hair grows back in or not. If you are one of the people who don't respond to laser treatment, you don't want to be stuck in a contract for expensive removal.

Weird factoid: The average single hair can carry the weight capacity of one single chocolate bar, without breaking.

2. Electrolysis. If performed correctly this is a wonderful form of permanent hair removal. The method used is a hair thin (very, very, very thin) metal probe is slid into a hair follicle. This does not puncture the skin. Electricity is generated through the probe, which destroys the hair. The history of electrolysis actually dates back to the Civil War when hair removal experimentation was recorded. Studies now show that 90% of women who seek electrolysis have satisfactory results. But you should employ a professional who comes with a good reference because even though electrolysis equipment is improved upon each year, the practitioner's skill is really the most important part. Your practitioner should be certified, but the truth is that most states don't regulate certification. In fact, approximately one third of all states do not require certification. If your practitioner is certified, they should display their certificate on the wall. So get a great recommendation from a friend or a doctor—who has had or seen good results before you invest.

Advantages:
* Permanency
* Looks good

Disadvantages:
* Expensive. Electrolysis is often charged by the minute, or block of time. For example $25 is charged for 15 minutes; $40 for 30 minutes and $60 for an hour.
*Tedious and difficult. If there are areas where there are large amounts of hair the process can take a long time. If this sounds like you, start with your underarms, or some other less hairy area, and then move on to hairier terrain.
* Re-growth. If done improperly, there can be a lot of re-growth of hair that you have to go back and have re-zapped. There can be skin damage.
* Pain. To alleviate pain you can choose your electrolysis intensity level. Having the current too low will alleviate any pain, but you may not get a good result, and will have to come back again for more treatment. Communicate with your practitioner to find the best balance between pain threshold and intensity level.

Factoid: Hair grows faster in warm weather and stretches in humidity.

Armpits
Underarms are a very sexy part of the body, not unlike the nape of your neck or your "knee pits." Keep them nice and smooth. Daily shaving, again, using the

same frequency and care you give your teeth, is a good standard. For a carefree summer, have your pits waxed. This is usually much less painful than a bikini wax. Check with your waxing technician about how much hair growth she needs you to have before you come in for an underarm waxing, in order to do a good job. In other words, don't shave your armpits before you come in for a treatment. There will be nothing for her to remove!

Make your life easier by buying a great magnifying mirror from your local beauty supply store. You can spot check different parts of your body more easily, rather than relying on standard bathroom or bedroom light and a wall mirror.

Pain relief tips for hair removal:
*Adrenalin and energy directly affect your pain levels. The more energy and adrenalin you have, the more pain you may feel. When you are calmer, you are less susceptible and aware of pain. Relax.
*Sugar and caffeine are stimulants that will make you more susceptible to pain and awareness of pain. Have some herbal tea.
* Schedule your hair removal around your menstrual cycle. Before your period your body may be more sensitive to pain.
*Medications may affect your pain level. If you take regular meds, check with your doctor and your practitioner about this.
*Ice and over the counter pain meds like Advil, Tylenol, etc. may help you as a pre-medication or an after medication. Check with your doctor and practitioner first.
*Tight jeans are not what you want to wear to your waxing appointment. After your waxing, your skin will be sensitive, and you don't want your jeans chafing your skin. The best thing to wear is a skirt with no underwear, or if you must, a G-string or thong to allow the most air and freedom from fabric friction on your freshly waxed skin. Just don't climb any ladders on your way home!
*Distract yourself. Try sucking on a piece of hard candy during your appointment to distract yourself.

Factoid: Female hair grows more slowly than male hair.

Hair is one of the sexiest differences between women and men. Men love lots of it on your head, and very little of it everywhere else. Maintain your hair because it is one of your greatest assets.

FUN FACTS:
Famous hairstyles and what they attracted:
Marge Simpson got Homer Simpson.
Veronica Lake got anyone she wanted.
Elvis Presley got Priscilla.
Louise Brooks got Charlie Chaplin.
Lady Godiva got everyone's attention.
Sampson got Delilah, and then he just got bald.
Cher got young, hot guys before Demi got Ashton.
Jennifer Anniston got famous, rich and she best of all, she got Brad.
The Bride of Frankenstein got Frankenstein.
Farrah Fawcett got Ryan O'Neill and that fabulous poster of herself to show her grandkids.
Shirley Temple got our hearts and a sweet drink named after her.
Dorothy Hammil got Warren Beatty and the gold medal.
Brooke Shields got Superman and Andre Agassi
Rapunzel got rescued because of her hair.

10

Oh, Make Me Over

The best thing is to look natural, but it takes makeup to look natural.

—Calvin Klein

Men don't like makeup, as a rule. But they do like you to look natural and polished, which usually involves make up that isn't so obvious. And successful, wealthy men do want you to fit in wherever they're going to take you—and if you play your cards right, they will be taking you to all kinds of restaurants, weekends, family and business affairs that will call for you to not just be presentable in everything from a casual to a formal look, but to be a standout.

In addition, makeup is part of your arsenal of weapons to create enchantment, because it can make you look more alluring and enticing, without looking garish. Think of makeup the way you do accessories for your clothing. Would you go out of the house without a pair of earrings on, or without your purse? Never. You know how the right pair of sunglasses can make your outfit look, so treat your mascara the same way. Besides, even for staying in the house—you should always aim to look good and that includes using make up—even when you're hanging around, because you just never know. Besides, makeup is fun. It's a creative endeavor like painting or cooking, and the right lip-gloss or shading of blush can make a man turn and stare at you with inspired wonder—although he's not sure why you look so good—he just knows you do, and that he'd like to spend more time with you.

"I love the confidence that makeup gives me."

—Tyra Banks

Skin

The most important thing you can do to get beautiful skin is to drink water—eight glasses a day—and get enough sleep. Stress in your life will show up in your skin. Another way you can improve your complexion is exercise. Getting the blood circulating and sweating out toxins will give your skin a beautiful and healthy glow. Sex is also great for your complexion—in addition to being fun, and a good workout!

Ways skin is negatively affected:
Stress
Hormones
Pollution
Sun
Smoking
Alcohol
Lack of sleep
Lack of exercise
Lack of hydration
Climate (windburn and chapped skin)
Medications
Over cleansing
Not removing makeup

Beautiful skin starts with clean skin. Always remove your makeup at night, even if you're exhausted. Cleanse your skin each evening. Over cleansing is one of the biggest mistakes women make, stripping their skin of natural moisture. Always clean your skin with a gentle cleanser and warm water.

Exfoliants that are gentle help get rid of dead skin, and dirt we can't see that clogs our pores. Scrubs, like exfoliants, are cleansers that contain particles like sand, or crushed fruit pits that perform the same function as exfoliants. As you clean your face, the particles gently massage and remove junk from your skin, and increase circulation. This can leave your skin glowing instead of dull.

> *I'm tired of all this talk about beauty being only skin deep. That's deep enough. Who wants an adorable pancreas?*
> —Jean Kerr

Toners, astringents and clarifying lotions should be applied with cotton balls to clean skin, and remove dirt and oil that your cleanser or exfoliant left behind.

Some of them are slightly harshly because they contain alcohol to chemically kill the germs. If you're sensitive, choose a non-alcohol based toner.

Masks are great deep cleaning or moisturizing treats for your skin once every two weeks. Always apply them to freshly cleaned skin.

Monthly facials can be wonderful treats for your skin if it is not too sensitive. Sometimes breakouts can follow a facial, so go makeup free for a few hours after your facial.

Pimples? Try the following tricks:
*A dab of toothpaste on the pimple before bed. Wash it off in the morning. The same ingredients that kill germs that cause cavities may just kill germs that cause breakouts.
*Calamine lotion
*Visine reduces the red from eyes—and zits.
*Preparation H reduces swelling—and not just you know where.
*Tea Tree oil

Moisturizers become more important the older you get. A special moisturizer for the eye area is important because the skin in that area is thinner and more sensitive than the rest of your face. If you purchase a moisturizer for your face, and you don't like the way it feels there, use it on your hands, or other parts of your body. A nighttime moisturizing cream will be a little heavier than daytime, and is only for those with dry skin.

Skin type tips:
Oily skin: Don't wear moisturizer or foundation when you exercise. As your pores open to release toxins, the moisturizer or foundation will invade the pores, and can clog or irritate them, causing breakouts. Exercise with a nude face. When you do use moisturizer, use one that is specialized for oily skin. When you exfoliate, don't overdo it just because your skin is oily. This will only aggravate and activate the oil glands. Treat breakouts with over the counter products. If your skin is problematic, see a dermatologist. Go to war on blackheads with regular deep cleaning facials.
Dry skin: Cleansers with milk in them are more nourishing than soaps, which can further dry already dry skin. Avoid toners with alcohol-based astringents.

Sensitive skin: Use jojoba and chamomile based products as well as hypoaller-genic and fragrance free items. Stay away from alcohol based toners. Milk based lotions or cleansers are nourishing. Vitamin E is wonderful for skin. You can take vitamin E capsules and pierce them with a pin and squeeze the oil from the cap-sules directly onto any scar tissues that you wish to give a more supple texture to. Vitamin E also heals chapped lips and ugly, dry cuticles.

> *"Anyone who keeps the ability to see beauty never grows old."*
> —Franz Kafka

Foundation must be well matched to your skin tone. Make sure that you always have good light when choosing and applying foundation. Experts recommend trying foundation close to your jaw line before you buy. If you can't try on the sample makeup in the store before you buy it, hold the bottle up to your jaw line, and get the best color match you can. Try to be near natural light because that is what most people will see you in when you wear the foundation.

> Tip: The mirror never lies! There is nothing worse than makeup that is not applied well and results in blotches. If something's wrong on your face, you want to be the one that catches it. Get a good magnifying make up mirror and have it in good, natural light for the best make up results.

Foundation evens out uneven skin one and can conceal small imperfections. It is also a source of sun protection, and you should make sure that your foundation has an SPF rating in it. That way you don't have to ruin your makeup with sun block over it. You should also make sure that your foundation is for oily, normal or dry skin, depending on what yours is. If you're not sure, ask a cosmetologist at your beauty salon or a department store makeup counter to help. If you have the correct foundation color, you won't be able to notice it. It should fade into your skin, and the look you present should be natural, but polished.

If you can't find a good foundation color match, consider custom blended foun-dation. Also, check and change foundation color seasonally as the weather changes the light around you, and your skin.

Foundation comes in different forms, so choose the type that is best for you. Here is some help:

*Liquid is good for all skin types.

*Crème foundation is thicker, and better for drier complexions. If it goes on too thick, you can use a damp makeup sponge to smooth and thin it. Crème foundation comes in a compact, as does a combination foundation that is part crème and part powder. This second type of compact foundation goes on wet, but dries to a powder. Watch out for crème foundation that accentuates eye lines when it dries.

*Stick foundation is fast to apply and great for covering scars, birthmarks or larger imperfections.

*And finally, the lightest foundations of all are tinted moisturizers and sheer face tint.

Lifespan of foundation: 1 year

Concealer should be one shade lighter than your natural skin tone, and is used for hiding blemishes or pimples that foundation doesn't take care of. Use a brush to apply concealer to imperfections, then a little foundation over that. Otherwise, use your fingertip to apply or blend it in with a sponge.

Again, concealer is sold in different forms. Pick the type that is best for you.

*Concealer sold in tubes gives light coverage.

* Liquids in a wand offer the very lightest texture and are good for quick repairs.

*Concealer sold in pencil sticks is good for pinpointing mini imperfections.

Trick: For puffy eyes try ice packs, cucumber slices, or moistened tea bags to draw out the toxins, or Preparation H to reduce swelling.

Lifespan of concealer: 1 year

Powder applied with a brush will lightly "set" your foundation, and keep it from smearing when you sweat during the day or night. Loose powder is lighter and more natural looking than pressed powder that comes in compacts. Loose powder also comes in a wider variety of colors and can be custom blended.

You can even use powder instead of foundation, but the drawbacks to loose powder is that it can be messy, and it isn't easy to carry around in your cosmetics bag. You can use loose powder at home, and carry a pressed powder in your purse for emergency fix ups in your purse. Make sure the two powders are as closely matched in color as possible.

Trick: When compact items crack or break—like powder or eye shadow or blush—simply crush them completely, put them in a container, and use them as powder.

Lifespan of powder: 1 year

Blush goes on the apples of your cheeks when you smile. Choose your blush shade by considering your skin color.
*Fair skin looks best in pinks.
*Medium skin looks best in warmer pinks with shades of brown in them
*Olive and yellow toned skin looks best in brown-based reddish plums

Blush usually comes in a crème form that you can apply with your fingers. This is great unless you have oily skin. Then you should use powder blush, which is applied with a brush. If you are going to mix blush colors to custom make your own, never mix the colors on your face.

Lifespan: Powder, 1 year; cream, 6–8 months.

Eyes are one of the most expressive parts of your face, and men love to stare into them. Foreplay starts with a look, a glance, or a sexy stare.

The Russians love Brooke Shields because her eyebrows remind them of Leonid Brezhnev.
—Robin Williams

Eyebrows make a huge difference on your face depending on how they are shaped. (Please tell me you pluck your eyebrows.) Using a good tweezers and good, natural light is important, as is not rushing or over plucking. A great magnifying mirror is also a perfect tool for your bathroom. Shaping the arch of the brow will give you a beautiful frame for your eyes.

Trick: Here is a pencil trick you can use to help shape your brows. Hold a pencil on the side of your nose. Your eyebrow should start at the tip of the pencil. Then hold the pencil diagonally, and extend it to the other end of your eye. That is where your brow should end. To determine where the arch should be highest, hold the pencil from the nostril to the outside edge of the iris—and that is the apex of your arch. Ideally, the inner edge of the brow should be equal to your nostril. The space between your brows should be equal to the width of your eye.

Before you start plucking, brush the eyebrow hair straight up. Never shave your eyebrows. If you'd like there is eyebrow mousse or gel to hold your eyebrows in place when you're done plucking. If you have an accident, and do over pluck, use a brow pencil to lightly color in the missing hair, until it grows in by itself.

For a quick fix, have your eyebrows professionally waxed or plucked. When you have your bikini line and legs waxed, have the waxing technician do your brows as well. It takes less than five minutes.

Eyeliner is always applied before eye shadow for a more natural look. Neutral tones are classic. Stay away from color that is too trendy and more likely, out of style. Felt tip eyeliners may be too severe on older eyes, and powder pencils give a shadowy look to eyes. Best are cream pencils or fat crayons, which are easy to use and can double as shadow. Liquid eyeliner is something you should save for your most dramatic looks.

Tip: If you have close set eyes, define the outer corners with eyeliner to draw attention outward. If you have narrow eyes, widen them by emphasizing the outer portion of the top lid and you can also line underneath with a thick, soft line.

Shimmering eye make up emphasizes wrinkles. And monochromatic looks like blue shadow with blue eyes, etc., are not as attractive as colors that give a little contrast to the actual eye color.

Eye shape, placement and color tricks:

*Small eyes—use eye shadow in light tones to give the impression of opening your eyes.

*Close set eyes—apply color to the outer corners to draw attention out and give the impression that your eyes are further apart. Another trick is to apply lighter shadow at the inner corner of each eye. Do the opposite for wide set eyes.

*Deep set eyes—light tones "open" the eye.

*Droopy eyes—a darker shadow towards the outer corners of the eyes is most flattering. Avoid color in the middle of the lid, which just emphasizes the droop.

> Tricks: Apply loose powder to your lid with a latex wedge before applying to increase staying power of eyeliner.

Chill your makeup pencils in the fridge or freezer before sharpening to avoid their breaking off.

> *The windows to the soul sometimes need window treatments.*
> —April Masini

Mascara should be the last makeup you apply. Apply one coat, let it dry then apply another. Start at the base of the lashes, wiggle the wand horizontally a few times, and then brush the wand out to the tips of your lashes. If you want to use an eyelash curler to curl your lashes up, apply your curler before you put on your mascara for 5–10 seconds. Do not wiggle or pull the curler while it is holding your lashes. Mascara color should be brown if your lashes are fair, or black if they're dark or if you want more contrast. Don't use brown, green, lavender, blue or anything else that's trendy. The waterproof type is great if you're going to have a cry in the movies or a swim in a pool.

> Trick: For fatter lashes, apply powder to closed eyes, and then apply mascara.

Hint: Straight wands are better than curved ones. The straight wands allow you to get to the small lashes in the corners of your eyes more easily.

Tip: Don't throw out your old mascara wands. Clean them in eye makeup remover, and keep them to remove clumps from lashes with too much mascara on them.

Mascara lifespan: Two to three months, tops.

Sex appeal is fifty percent what you've got and fifty percent what other people think you've got.
—Sophia Loren

Your smile has two components: Teeth and lips.

The biggest improvement you can make to your appearance is making sure your teeth are white and that has never been easier than today. Tooth color is genetic. Some people are just born with yellow tinted teeth. But certain foods and beverages can be avoided to keep teeth whiter. They are coffee, red wine and tea. Any foods that stain your clothes will stain your teeth. If your teeth are naturally yellow, you will get a big positive yield out of whitening your teeth. Teeth whitening can be undertaken at home or at your dentist's office. The home products are reasonably priced, but require some discipline to apply the whitener, not eat after it is on, and remove it in the morning—for about three weeks. Dentists can perform various teeth whitening procedures that are usually about $500 and not covered by insurance, but are quick! (Often in one or two visits.)

Lips should look inviting and kissable, so after taking good care of them by making sure there is no dead skin on them, and regularly maintaining them with vitamin E or balm, make sure they look polished and soft.

•Matte lipstick is strong on color without shine, but can be drying and look dull. If you like the matte look, get a good, expensive lipstick. This is one type where cheap isn't better.
*Crème—nice color without shininess, and more moisturizing than matte
*Glossy—the least drying

Lip shape tricks:
*Lips too full? Avoid strong colors or you'll look like Ronald McDonald. Tone down the color with softer, sheerer hues and no lip liner. Also, play up your eyes to draw away from or balance out your full lips.
*Lips too thin? Strong colors will just emphasize their thinness. Instead, use lighter, sheer colors. Never use lip liner outside the natural lip line to try and fake bigger lips. You'll just end up looking like a clown.
*Crooked lips? Gently use your lip liner to even them out.

Time may be a great healer, but it's a lousy beautician.
—Unknown

Lip color depends on your skin tone as well as your clothing colors:
*Best lip colors for fair skin: pales
*Best lip colors for medium skin: deeper colors
*Best lip colors for olive and yellow skin: browns and plums
*Best lip colors for dark skin: dark red, beiges and berry colors

Makeup Supplies:
Like a well-stocked closet, you want your bathroom to have all the supplies you need to make yourself beautiful, in order. Do inventory and re-stock every month. This is your treasure chest. Men detail their cars with meticulous care. You must make sure you makeup supplies are as cared for. Online beauty supply companies make the shopping easy.

*Brushes. You should have a collection of brushes that you can use for eye shadows, foundation, powder, blush and eyeliner. You should also have a brow brush—a clean toothbrush works fine.
*Cotton swabs
*Eyelash curler
*Tweezers—invest in a great pair
*Sharpener—separate sharpeners for lip, eye or concealer pencils and crayons.
*Latex cosmetic wedges

Trick: Purchase makeup brushes in a good art supply store—much cheaper and good quality.

And last but not least—now that you have this beautiful face, not just naturally beautiful, but beautifully made up, too, use it! Laugh! Smile! Send a million flirtatious looks—and enchant him.

INTERESTING STATISTICS:

According to a February 2004 MSNBC.com poll, of 15,000 people surveyed, three quarters of whom were men, with an average age of 38, and the women surveyed having an average age of 34, and approximately two thirds of all of them had bachelor's degrees from college, and over 90% considered themselves to be straight:

* Two thirds of the women and over half of the men had logged onto a personals site.

* Of those who logged on, 44% of the women and 33% of the men said the got more dates, more sex and more long lasting love as a result of using online personals.

* Women in their 40s seem to have the best luck with online dating because they are more in control of online dating than other kinds of dating.

* Ten percent of women admit to being less than truthful about their weight or appearance in online dating, but 72 percent of men and women say they do not lie about their appearance at all.

· 11

There's No Body Like
A Hot Body

"Our bodies are our gardens—our wills are our gardeners."
—William Shakespeare

Sure, men may say that they love women of all shapes and sizes, but the truth is that most men—especially rich and successful men—want to date a woman who is fit—NOT fat. You may be able to hide some of your figure flaws with your wardrobe, but since so much of the fun in a relationship happens when the clothes come off, you don't want body issues to come between you and bedroom business. Moreover, a fit and thin woman in the dating world has infinitely more possibilities than an overweight woman. Sorry, but that's the truth, and that's what I'm here to tell you—whether you like it or not.

Consider this:

*A Cornell University study found that men have less tolerance for dating overweight partners than women do, and the men consistently report less comfort in dating overweight women.

*A recent women's magazine poll found that 50 percent of men wouldn't even consider dating a woman they deemed overweight. More than one-third of the men in the same poll said they would end a relationship with their current girlfriend if she gained too much weight.

The fact is that men just aren't attracted to overweight women, and if a man doesn't feel that attraction, he can't get an erection. Without an erection, a man can't have sex, and without sex, a man just doesn't feel like a man, and he will look for a woman who does make him feel like a man. Sex is just more important to men than it is to women, and sex in a relationship is more important to men than it is to women. So making yourself sexually appealing in a relationship is just good common sense. When you look at it that way, you can see that your appearance plays a huge role in reinforcing his manhood and your relationship. That may seem like a lot of pressure on you to stay in shape, but in the end, isn't it worth it to have a healthy sex life? Without a doubt it is. There are two main ways to take care of your body: 1) Diet or what you put into your mouth and 2) Exercise or what you do with your body and how you keep it running.

A 2003 New England Journal of Medicine study showed evidence that may link regular exercisers with more frequent sexual activity than non-exercisers.

The Daters Diet

Everybody wants a quick fix but they're not just hard to find—when you do find them, ultimately they usually are too good to be true. There is, however, a simple way to fix up your diet that will help you get healthy and lose weight. Healthy nutrition, clear, glowing skin, shiny hair, and a small waist line are attainable by simply mastering the three Cs: color, carbs and calories, and by learning to add and subtract six.

If you're on a date, and you have a choice between the sumptuous buffet and ordering off the menu—choose to order off the menu, it doesn't come with seconds.

—April Masini

April, Cavemen and Carbs

For years, I've had women (and men) asking me 'how do you stay so thin"? Well, I'll tell you…and in honesty, the answer is as old as man himself….

When it all began, we were hunter-gatherers and we existed on wild game, fish and shellfish, plus a seasonal variety of wild vegetables, fruits, seeds and nuts. These pre-agricultural diets rarely contained concentrated carbohydrate sources such as sugar, flour, bread, rice and pasta—the white and beige colored foods. Cavemen and women liked a lot of color in their diets—and if you want to be a slender, sexy siren—so should you!

Start with this test: The next time you look down at your plate, or your shopping cart, notice what colors you see. If you see lots of beige and white food, you need a color overhaul. When all of the food you're eating is white or beige, it's pretty much guaranteed to be full of sugar, full of simple carbohydrates, and therefore, full of calories. Not only that, but it takes bigger portions of these colorless foods to make you feel satisfied and full. It's a no-win eating situation. It's time to add some green(s)—yellow, red, orange, purple and blue—any hue will do, as long as it's natural.

In fact, the American Dietetic Association upped their requirements from five to nine servings of fruits and vegetables per day and has its own reasons for recommending a colorful diet. Colorful fruits and vegetables contain vitamins, fiber, heart-healthy ingredients, and cancer- and disease-fighting antioxidants. In addition, eating fruit and vegetables as the basis of each meal is a guaranteed method of controlling weight. And most fruits and vegetables are low in calories and fat and contain lots of water and fiber to help you feel full faster.

My solution is a simple one, (1) try as best you can to eliminate processed and packaged food from your diet and (2) make an effort to replace them with fruit, vegetables, meat and fish…. In other words, don't mess with Mother Nature!

April's Secret Math Equation to Her Size 6: Add 6 and Subtract 6 to be A (Size) 6

While I, personally, can gain weight very easily, I've managed to maintain my size 6 figure my entire adult life. How? Not by any of the popular, trendy, diets. I don't think they work long term, and studies show that nearly all, eventually, gain everything they lost back—and then some. My weight loss and weight management solution is very simple, but it requires me to live a dedicated life style. On the other hand, it works and the result lasts. All you are required to do is add six food items to your diet, while you deduct six others…it's as simple as that. You can do this as quickly or as slowly as you want, but the sooner you make these additions and deductions, the faster you'll see results. In fact, every single person I know who's followed my plan has seen results in as little as two weeks.

The greatest wealth is health.

—Virgil

April's 6 Foods To Add:

1. Protein—at every meal. That's right, return to the caveman days. The best protein to have is fish (any kind) three to four times a week, with lean beef, pork, chicken, lamb, eggs, etc., filling in the rest. By the way, fried (anything) does *not* count.

2. Nuts—any kind you like, but no more than a quarter-cup at a time and no more than half a cup a day. Nuts are packed with protein and "the good fats" and are my #1 snack choice.

3. Fiber—in the form of vegetables, fruits and beans…not only will these foods keep you 'regular' (if you know what I mean) but fiber is also very filling.

4. Raw vegetables—they are rich in vitamins, minerals and enzymes—few things (other than lots of water and great sex) can produce as healthy looking hair and skin. And, yes, raw, freshly made vegetable juice definitely counts.

5. Berries—My favorites! Berries are beneficial beyond belief and could fill this page singing their praises, besides the fact that they are tasty. Trust me, on this one.

6. Calcium Supplement—I like the soft calcium chews, especially the caramel and chocolate.

April's 6 Foods To Subtract:

1. Pasta—none, period. So long, spaghetti.

2. Bye-bye bread—If you must indulge, make it authentic whole-grain bread, but even then, please, no more than one to two slices daily, tops.

3. Sugar (white and brown)—Sayonara to anything with five or more grams of sugar (per serving).

4. Sodas and pre-sweetened juices—these are almost solid sugar (often labeled glucose, dextrose, corn syrup, glucose syrup, high fructose corn syrup) a.k.a. high calorie count, empty calories. Adios sweet drinks.

5. Packaged cookies, cakes, pies, crackers and desserts. I know, I know, I know…I have a huge sweet tooth myself, but try it for two weeks and see what happens. If you must indulge, go for the Angel Food cake instead of the Devil's Food with Frosting. Or bake sweets yourself, and limit the amount of sugar you use. You can replace white sugar with honey, and only use half the amount!

6. Dairy—low fat cheese or skim milk on occasion is okay, but try to stick with soy products.

April on Food Shopping and Restaurant Ordering: "Bigger is Better"
Portion control is a major problem for many people. Most restaurant servings are two to three times a healthful portion size, which means dining out often may cause you to be two to three sizes bigger than you should be. Super sizing at fast food restaurants has led to super sized waistbands, and the buying-in-bulk shopping trend inspired by wholesale warehouse stores has perpetuated the American ideal that bigger is better and more is majestic. The only things you should buy at these stores are light bulbs and paper towels—not food! Let me tell you, that motto may hold true for some things (I hope I don't need to mention what things I'm referring to!), but your dress size is not one of them. My solution: leave a third of your food on your plate or ask for a half order.

> *If fitness came in a bottle, everyone would have a great body.*
> —Cher

More Math: Weight Maintenance vs. Weight Loss
The basic guide to determining how many calories you should be consuming in a day is to determine your basal metabolic rate (BMR), which is the number of calories that your body needs to perform its daily functions. Do this by multiplying your weight by the number 10. (A 140-lb. woman should consume roughly 1,400 calories per day if she wants to maintain weight.) Obviously, this number will vary depending on your activity level. The scale is as follows:

Multiply BMR by the following to incorporate activity factor:

- Sedentary: BMR x 1.3

- Light activity: BMR x 1.5

- Moderate activity: BMR x 1.7

- Heavy activity: BMR x 1.9

Now that we know how much we need to eat to maintain our weight, we equally need to understand what it takes to lose weight at a healthy rate of one to two pounds per week—that is, cutting 250–500 calories from your daily diet—or you can burn them away.

A study on exercise and first impressions published in the Journal of Sport and Exercise Psychology found that unlike non-exercisers, who were perceived to be sickly, scrawny or lumpy and sexually unattractive. People who exercised regularly were perceived as healthy, muscular and sexually attractive. What's even better about exercise is that it not only gives you a body that is sexually appealing, it actually has been proven to improve your sex life. Studies have found that women who exercise build endurance, which improves duration and frequency of sex. Even better news from researchers at the University of Texas, Austin, who found that exercise increases blood flow to all the muscles, including the ones down below, boosting women's vaginal responses by 169 percent after a workout. This tells me that not only should you be exercising, you should be having sex immediately after leaving the gym. (Or even at the gym, if the right partner is available. But you didn't hear that from me.)

Weight Training
Time and again, women tell me they avoid lifting weights for fear of bulking up and looking like The Governator. Let's clear up the confusion once and for all: Forget your fears of becoming too bulky. It rarely happens with women and only in genetically gifted specimens who train for a living. Moreover, weight training gives your muscles tone and shape and is your best ally in fat burning. Here's why: Most of your calories are burned in the power centers of the muscle cells. The more muscle you have, the more of these fat-burning power plants you have working for you. So, while it's true that some women have more muscle than others, it is unlikely that without pharmaceutical enhancement you'll end up looking like Girly-Men.

There are strength-training exercises for all of the major muscle groups and working out all muscle groups evenly will produce the best results. Start a strength training routine by doing one set of 8 to 12 repetitions of one particular muscle group. Once you feel comfortable that you're doing the exercise correctly, you can add more sets—and weight.

When considering a sport to take up, consider this factoid: Percentage of runners who say they think about sex while running: 66%.

Calorie Cutting Cardio
A cardiovascular workout is defined as any activity "used, designed or performed

to cause a temporary increase in heart rate." Going by that definition, a night of good sex or the discovery of a Gucci sample sale could be considered a cardio workout. Even though both may leave you feeling spent, and one is guaranteed to leave you lighter in the wallet, neither will leave you with a firmer butt or well toned thighs. Those results require cardio that's a lot less instantly gratifying, but gives you a lot more long-term satisfaction.

Get off the cardio machines—that's my first tip for all you gym-goers. Every time I'm at the gym, I see the same group of women stepping up and down for hours, only to reach the same plateau—of weight, that is. Stairmasters and elliptical machines may be helpful for overweight women who are easing their way back into exercise, but I've got to tell you—they keep bopping up and down, but their bodies never seem to change.

Jump on the treadmill instead, and, if it all possible, do it on an incline (it's great for your butt)! Beginners can alternate walking for two minutes and jogging for one minute for a duration of 30 minutes; more advanced exercisers can adjust the incline and alternate jogging and sprinting.

Take your calorie burning cardio elsewhere: outdoors, to the swimming pool, jump rope, or to a group class for kickboxing, spinning, or even aerobic strip tease (Yes, it can be a workout, just ask Carmen Electra—or better yet, her husband!). While we're on the topic of burning…Forget about the fat-burning zone: When trying to burn calories, work as hard as you can for as long as you can, so long as you don't cause injury or burnout. The idea that you will only lose fat if you work in some magic "zone" is simply untrue. If you enjoy working at the lower intensities, make sure you compensate by going longer.

Never eat more than you can lift.

—Miss Piggy

Here are a few more ways to boost your calorie killing cardios:

- Eliminate the elevator: Take the stairs everywhere. In fact, take two steps at a time. Skipping a step will force your leg and buttocks muscles to extend and work harder. Plus, this movement releases endorphins that will make you feel great!

- Put on your dancing shoes: The bar scene isn't the best place to pick up men or to burn calories. Push the barstool aside and hit the dance floor instead. An hour of social dancing can burn more than 300 calories.

- Save gas and burn fuel: Instead of hopping in your car to run every errand, walk to nearby stores.

- Take more steps: Don't fight for the closest parking spot at the mall. Park as far away as possible and walk briskly through the parking lot—and the food court. Better yet, bypass it altogether. In the office, walk to your co-worker's cubicle to talk, don't pick up the phone or resort to instant messaging.

- Do yard work. Pull weeks, dig holes, rake leaves, and mow your lawn. Gardening just one hour can burn up to 500 calories.

- Burn calories while doing housework. Do several chores at one time. For instance, make the bed, put laundry in the dryer, run upstairs to fold clean clothes and put them away. When you're making the beds, keep your shoulders back and pretend you have a book on your head. While you're dusting, roll up on the balls of your feet to work your calves.

No matter how you look at it, exercise is key. It trims, tones, tightens and turns you—and your partner—on. Now, what are you waiting for? Get off the couch and get moving! There's plenty of time to use that couch for other activities after your workout.

And a few more ways to cut cravings:

1. **Reach for water before you reach for a snack.** It's the cheapest, safest appetite suppressant there is.

2. **Use spices liberally.** Ginger, cayenne, jalapeno peppers and Tabasco sauce can boost your fat-burning ability by up to 25%, according to a researcher at Kyoto University in Japan.

3. **Sleep for weight loss.** Getting enough sleep does more than keep you from eating for energy. The University of Chicago recently found that a woman's metabolism rises 40% when she gets enough sleep. Obesity and sleep loss are related in certain studies.

4. **Follow the pros' lead.** To get fit fast, models cut out the ABCs—alcohol, bread, and complex carbohydrates.

5. **Beat nighttime cravings.** Researchers have found that dark rooms and the darkness of night make us more likely to overeat. Try scheduling your bedtime for an hour earlier. If you have a favorite program that you like to watch at night, tape it to watch at a different time. Switch to brighter light bulbs for cheerier surroundings, you'll be happier and less likely to binge.

6. **Snack right.** A hard candy is only about 20 calories and can last up to twenty minutes. A 400-calorie ice cream cone never lasts more than ten minutes.

INTERESTING STATISTICS:

Cyber Dating, Cyber Sex

According to a May 2004 MSNBC.Com article, 40 million Americans log onto personals sites monthly. Their February 2004 survey of over 15,000 people reported that:

73 % of women who have gone on dates that were arranged through online dating sites, have slept with one or more of their dates.

Women who cyber date report more dates.
Men who cyber date report more sex.

17% of those surveyed said that they looked at online porn with a partner.

12

Clothes That Will Get You Close To Him

Good clothes open all doors

—Thomas Fuller

Clothes are one of a vixen's great tools. She uses them to make herself more seductive and enticing. She creates an image that will startle and attract men by using clothes that enhance her own specific loveliness. Every woman needs a closet full of the right clothes—whether you're committed to seducing a man with a closet full of sensual, sexy lingerie and evening wear, or winning an election with clothes that sell your political sensibility (and subliminal sexuality) or you want to get out of a speeding ticket (come on Ladies, you know cops are vulnerable) with a pretty, vulnerable look. Any man and woman who really wants something and gets it, knows how important clothes are to the process.

Think about all the successful women you know, and how they dress, and you'll see I'm right. Everyone I talked about in the chapter on confidence uses clothes like a second skin. Now try some man-think. Would a builder leave his house without a hardhat and overalls, not to mention the proper saw, hammer, nails, screws, etc.? No, because he wants to do his job well and he needs these clothes and tools to do it. Would you hire a builder who showed up looking like anything *but* what I've just described? No, you wouldn't, because you have an idea in your head of what a good builder looks like, and that's what you want. Would a doctor see patients without looking professional and responsible in a suit under his white coat, and those very good shoes on his feet, let alone operate without the best scalpel? No, because he's doing his job well, and he's selling you his professionalism. Assuming all doctors have graduated medical school, and passed their medical board exams, you have a choice as a patient, just like men have a choice in the women they choose. You will pick a doctor that you feel is successful—and men will pick a woman they feel is successful at being sexual and feminine and enticing. You will base your decision partly on their reputation, but mostly (because most doctors have a good reputation, so that alone doesn't weed out the one who is right for you), based on how you feel about them, personally. One last example to hammer the point home: Would you take your car to a mechanic change your oil and replace your brake pads, if he didn't have any grease on his clothes? No—because you'd think, this guy doesn't know what he's doing. To be good with cars, a mechanic has to get dirty to get deep inside the bowels of an oily engine under the hood. If this mechanic isn't dirty, he must not be getting under the hood, and he must be a quack.

Why do women sometimes think of clothes differently then these men think of their own garb? There are several reasons. Sadly, some of us have been taught to think of clothes as frivolous luxuries that we don't deserve because they're visceral and material, and therefore bad values, instead of thinking of them as useful tools. That is because our true femininity and womanliness, our inner vixens, have been denied, ignored and repressed. This has hurt us, and men. Materialism has gotten an umbrella definition that doesn't serve us—there really is a difference between clothes that you need to do something (like get a man) and clothes that you buy and never wear. When you truly think of your clothes as tools, they won't seem frivolous. They'll seem necessary. The clothes that you actually use to entice are just as important a tool as your car that gets you places and your food that powers you through the day. Clothes that you buy and never wear because they were not well thought out purchases—those are material mistakes, and quite literally bad values, and should not be repeated. The right clothes are not frivolous. They're necessary.

Then there are those mothers and women who have taught us to think of clothes the same way we think of sweets—they're wonderful things, and it's okay to treat yourself to them once in a while, but it's better to spend your time and money on a good book to improve your mind. Well, wake up call, ladies! This is a good book and it's improving your mind, and I'm telling you to go shop for an arsenal of clothes that you can use to seduce and enchant a man! Your mind and your body are inter-related. Sure, a great mind is terrific, but it's enormously and exponentially terrific if it comes in a great body! Remember, seduction begins with a man's mind—and it starts with your mind, too. But it doesn't end there. Your body and your clothes are key—as is your personality, your manners, your congeniality and your grace.

Fashions fade, style is eternal.

—Yves Saint Laurent

Okay, here's my last pitch to try and change your old thinking into new and improved thinking about dating men: If you're still believing the idea that says, "What kind of a brat would I be shopping for clothes when there are starving children in the world to feed?" well, I'll tell you. If you can use your wardrobe full of beautiful clothing to get the successful and wealthy man you want, you will be more apt and better equipped financially to take care of starving children than he is! If you take care of yourself, you can take care of others. Think about it.

Now that you understand that clothes are essential, pulling together a full proof look, and stocking your closet so you never have to utter those four words, "What Should I Wear?" again, is going to be easy after you read this chapter. Keep in mind that the goal is to have something to wear all the time that is not only right for any occasion, but also for your body, and your best look. Clothes should flatter your figure and attract the men you want. Having the right clothes, and wearing them at the right times is all part of selling your dating-self. Only it's two-fold. You want to attract wealthy, successful men, but you also want to give yourself that inner happiness and ease that spells confidence and sexiness from within. Clothes can do both of these things for you.

The way we dress tells people, and men in the case of this book, an enormous amount about ourselves. Our clothes declare us joyful, curious, sensitive, happy, feminine, creative, assured or, on the other hand, lacking in imagination, insecure, timid, boring or slobs. Your clothes are extensions of your personality. They must fit your form, compliment your lines, and flatter you with their colors. All the clothes you wear should complement each other, because you are aiming for an overall harmonious and beautiful effect, therefore, organizing, assessing and purchasing your clothing go hand in hand. So let's get down to brass tacks and get to work.

Organizing, assessing & purchasing

To begin, understand the goal is to create a small but quality wardrobe that is carefully planned and that will with stand the test of time. This means you should just say no to any super trendy clothes or accessories. Throw out or give away your un-wearable clothes. Pull out any and all clothes you don't wear because they're too long, too short, too tight or too baggy, and alter them.

Next, consider your closet. Treat it like a sacred space, or treat it with the same TLC that men treat their coveted cars and garages. Your closet is a place you go to several times a day to choose what you're going to put on your body, yet it is often a space that is disregarded. As a result, you often enter or look into your closet with a lack of energy. It should be a space that inspires you, not sucks the life out of you. Spruce up the space and you'll notice how much more you enjoy going to the closet and how much more creative you'll be at choosing your clothes. Organize your closet with care. Arrange your closet by seasons, and then by colors. Keep the pants in one area, and the skirts in another. Invest in good hangers. Padded hangers for delicate garments and pant and skirt hangers with clips that won't bunch your clothing while it's hanging as well as hangers that accommodate pants and a jacket, and have a tier to hang another garment, like a blouse on it also, so you can create outfits that will save you time choosing.

Tip: If you don't have a lint brush, try wrapping a piece of scotch tape around your hand a couple of times, sticky side up. Run the sticky side up and down your clothing, and voila! Lint and fuzz are gone.

Keep matching accessories (belts, scarves, jewelry and gloves) on the same hangers or nearby the clothes they're worn with. Hang a rack on your closet wall that you can hang belts, scarves and hats on. Decide if you'd rather have your shoes in a hung shoe bag, or on a multi-tiered rack that sits on the floor. Clear plastic shoe boxes are also great space savers as long as you tape a photo of the shoes onto the end of the box, so you don't have to open each box to see what's inside every time you're choosing shoes.

Only after you've organized what you own and actually wear can you decide if, and what, you need to buy. Mentally review the routine of your life and see what items of clothing you really lack. Compose a clear picture in your mind. Always keep the basic questions in mind: What do you really need? How much can you spend for it?

Choose basic clothes in a popular price range that give wide possibility for individuality. Start by thinking about styles that are simple, exciting but understated, that fit into your life and that you can make truly your own by the way you accessorize them. This calls for dresses and suits that are classically cut, with unbroken, uncluttered lines-clothes which challenge your imagination to add your own kind of special touches: a scarf tied at the side of a round neckline, arresting jewelry and color-complementary shoes and bags. Basic clothing must fit into your life because it can be dressed up or down, and because it automatically sees you through a day that begins with shopping and ends with cocktails.

A non-fussy, gadget-free wardrobe is the golden rule to live, shop and dress by. This may seem to be another way of saying what I've just said, but there are women who are seduced by dresses decorated with rhinestones, sequins, bows, feathers or heaven-knows-what. Millions of those plastic pocketbooks with gaudy appliques have been sold. There are hats that look like a double banana split and which the women who buy them often wear with heavy doses of make-up, jewelry, and furs. My advice in such cases: PLEASE, ladies, don't compete with the circus. No successful, wealthy man wants to date a fashion don't.

> *Only great minds can afford a simple style.*
> —Stendhal

Classics and neutrals vs. colors in your closet
Yes, I believe in investing in classic wardrobe, but not a wardrobe devoid of color! Look, there is a reason Paris and Florence, the two ruling cities of fashion, have been showing collections that are alive with color for years…sun yellow, bright blues, vivid orange, blazing pinks. Ladies, if you are one of those people who is sticking to a few "safe colors" in which you feel sure no one can possibly accuse you of being garish, or of seeking too much attention—listen up!

How and why to use color
a) All sorts of tests have proved that men, (not unlike bulls) are responsive to color. Green is reputedly soothing, violet is cooling, blue is thoughtful, pink is provocative; red is stimulating, yellow is healing.

b) Colors can accent and mold your figure when used skillfully, by highlighting certain areas, and low lighting others.

c) Color creates illusion. A girl in an icy-blue and white dress, provided the rest of her is well kept, immediately creates an impression that is pleasing to the eye. A spring-green is uplifting, and seems fresh and happy. White is traditionally, but also visually, pristine, pure and clean. Though against a deep tan, if the dress includes a daring neckline, it becomes undeniably sexy. Black is sophisticated and chic-though it can also seem somber and depressing to some people. Pink is a young color-maybe a bit too sweet on older women. The bottom line is color is an important part of the image you create.

d) Color blindness affects men more than it does women. This means that he may see navy, black, hunter-green and dark gray as one in the same. Yellow, red or lavender do not get confused in colorblind men the way darker neutrals or darker shades with blue or green in them, do. So get him to notice you by wearing a color he can actually see!

Color in clothing works best when it's working with the color in your skin and not against it. Fashion and color experts say that almost all skins fall into one of three skin-color groups: 1) cool—have blue undertones; 2) warm—have yellow undertones; and 3) neutral—have pink to beige undertones. If your skin falls into the cool range, the best colors for you will be those that have some hint of blue in them—like violets, blue-reds, blue-greens, and whites. Warm skins should benefit most from colors near those reds and greens that have yellowish sunny shades to them. The neutral skins are free to wear either group for the best look. Hold different colors up to your face in good, natural light, and see which colors are most flattering, then figure out which skin tone you are, cool, warm or neutral.

So, remember, when thinking about color, the following rules apply:
1. Simplicity to start. The over-all look of any outfit should be dominated by one color. This is true no matter how many touches of different colors you may add.
2. Catch his eye with color. Touches of white on a dark outfit give the effect of a neon light on a dark street. Shiny, black beading or any light-reflecting fabrics beckon attention.
3. Avoid visual clutter that takes his attention away from you.
4. Buy clothes that are modern and utilitarian to get the most use. I think the new fabrics with their permanent pleats, easy travel-ability, non-ironing, quick wash, quick-dry talents have changed many of the old rules about basic clothing, and have enormously enlarged the scope and possibility of what we can wear. For

instance, everyone's heard of the new wonder material "Lycra"; the best part about it is that it's light, and it withstands daily rough use.

I wear my sort of clothes to save me the trouble of deciding which clothes to wear.

—Katharine Hepburn

Once you understand color you need to understand lines
1. Vertical lines are slimming. A dress with one long line will be more slimming than a skirt and blouse that "cuts" you in the middle.
2. You can use color to create the illusion of one line. For example, a skirt and blouse in one color, will give the appearance of one long line, and are therefore, almost as slimming as a simple-lined dress, while a skirt and a blouse in two different colors will "cut" you in the middle, taking away to the long line. Prints and stripes do not take away from slimming looks. Seams, button closings, sleeve endings, and all details and decorations as well as any striped prints or fabrics can "break up" a clean line.
3. Horizontal lines are broadening. If you have a small bust and want to give the illusion of a larger one, wear stripes up top. Stripes down below will give you a broader backside look, which is something you normally want to avoid. Any stripes or patterns on fabrics that run horizontally, will give you a broader, wider look.
4. Diagonal lines are universally flattering—not just on the fabric, but in the cut of a piece of clothing.
5. Unorganized detail or clutter distracts his eye. If he's too busy looking at your fashion design of an outfit, he won't notice you, so make sure that you present a unified, organic image. Not a mish mash of too many different looks. Remember, you want him to be looking at you—that is what your clothing is for, to enhance you and your beauty.
6. Light draws attention and as such may be fattening—or if you need some weight gain, flattering. If you have a great body lights can be quite flattering. If you do choose to wear white, consider a monochromatic look with a dash of color somewhere other than your waistline.
7. Dark de-emphasizes and "thins" you to your slimmest look.

Don't shop till you drop—shop smart
Shopping is a process—you will accrue all of the pieces you need in your ward-

robe over time—not in one trip to the mall. Even so, make sure you've eaten, and are well rested so you can make clothing purchases as carefully as you would do your taxes or make a souffle. Don't shop when you're in a rush. You'll make bad choices. Try to shop on "off" hours. Weekday mornings are the best because there are smaller crowds. Shop early in the season for selection, and shop late in the season for bargains. And remember: think about what you really need for your particular life, as you want it to be, and how much you can afford.

Here's what I think you need in your closet so that you're ready for anything:
1. A black dress. Although there's no solid evidence that cavewomen had them, little black dresses are historical must haves because they are charming and enchanting. If it's well fitted and simple in design, it will be one of the most important pieces in your closet. One thing you can count on with this item: Nothing says classy like a black dress and pearls. It's fashion eternity.
Choose a dress that can be chameleon-like. A perfect basic dress has one kind of chic in the morning—it can be worn with flat heels, sporty scarves and belts—and a second kind of chic in the evening, when the same dress accompanied by richer jewelry, stiletto heels and an elegant wrap should be literally unrecognizable as the same dress you wore at 11 a.m. The key to your choice lies in its simplicity. Learn to recognize it when you see it; a simple top, a clear plain neckline, the skirt slim or slightly flared, as little detail as possible, and preferably in a solid color.

> *Fashion is a kind of vitamin for style.*
>
> —Yves Saint Laurent

2. A great pair of trousers. Katherine Hepburn knew this before the rest of us. A great, wonderfully fitting pair of trousers (light wool for winter, cotton blend for summer) is a must have. Pick a solid color like black, navy, brown, sage, camel, cream or snow white. Yes, white wool is one of the great winter treasures.
Take time to make sure these fit well. Well fitting trousers flatter figures that are overweight or need some weight. The pants shouldn't pull across the abdomen or squeeze your waist. And at the bottom of the pant leg, these trousers should hit your shoe at the top of the arch. If they don't—tailor them!

How to find a good tailor:

1. Ask the store where you purchase your trousers if they tailor their own stock. If they do, you're set. If they don't, ask them to recommend someone.

2. Ask your friends. Personal references are great resources.

3. Find one in your neighborhood and ask to meet the tailor. Often local dry cleaning establishments have a tailor on the premises or one who comes in several days a week. Ask them what they think of the item and the job, and if they've ever worked on items like yours. Ask them how much it will cost and how long it will take.

4. Call a local designer boutique or the couture department of your highest end department store, like Neiman's, Barney's or Saks, and ask them to recommend a tailor.

5. Fabric and textile stores often will give you a referral to a tailor.

Having pants tailored usually costs five to twenty five dollars depending on how much work you need done, and is worth every penny. Trousers that don't quite fit should not be worn. It's harsh, but think of it as fashion tough love. You want to look great, and clothes that *almost* look right will leave you *almost* looking right—and that's not good enough. Having pants tailored also helps establish a relationship with a tailor. This can be as valuable as your relationship with your hairdresser or your gynecologist. Let your tailor get to know your body and your clothes and how you like things to fit. This will take some communication. Some tailors naturally like to fit things snuggly, and unless you are articulate and specific, will do so. Other tailors like to fit things with more breathing room which may be roomier than you'd like. So, speak up and say what you like.

On matters of style, swim with the current; on matters of principal, stand like a rock.

—Thomas Jefferson

---

3. A good pair of jeans. Not the beat-up old ones. You need a new pair that you can wear with a tee shirt or a blazer. These jeans should work for a casual date, a Saturday afternoon of antique shopping in the country, casual Friday at your office or his nephew's Gymboree birthday party. Certain brands will make your butt look more rounded. Other pairs make your legs look longer or your stomach flatter. The fabric and the cut can make your body look better or worse than it actually is. NEVER turn your jeans into sausage casing, and make your body the

sausage! The worst possible thing you can do is to wear a pair of jeans that are too tight. Nothing is more of a visual turnoff to men, or more likely to get you a yeast infection, than a pair of jeans that you are stuffed into. If you gain weight or shrink your jeans, put them away or give them to charity and buy the next size. Sorry, it's more fashion tough love.

4. A skirt. One good skirt that stops just above the knee is a must have. A great style of skirt is a modified pencil skirt. A classic shape, with or without a small slit for movement—and for showing off your legs—that falls just above your knee, in a solid color, is alluring. You can pair it with a blazer, a V-neck sweater, a turtle-neck, or a blouse—the sky is pretty much the limit and he'll love looking at your legs.

5. A blazer. This is an important purchase. The best ones will last for years and years. Choose a name brand to make sure you get a great fit, and pick a classic color like navy, camel or black. Make sure the blazer fits your waist and trunk, and is not too roomy. You don't want to 'swim' in it. Not flattering. It also shouldn't pull across the waist or chest when buttoned. Sleeves should hit the crease in your arm where your wrist meets your arm. If it doesn't—take it to the tailor! And be sure that the blazer looks good on you buttoned and unbuttoned.

Extra tip: A leather blazer is a great extra to add to your wardrobe. A fitted one is perfect. Leave the bombers and the motorcycle jacket styles to the men. You can wear a leather blazer pretty much anywhere you can wear a wool blazer. If in doubt, wear the wool one, as of the two, that is the more classic, and classic is never wrong. But for fun night dates—like the amusement park, bowling, movies and a Chinese restaurant, a leather blazer and jeans is totally hot.

Fashion is architecture: it is a matter of proportions.
—Coco Channel

6. A white cotton shirt blouse (with a little Lycra). A beautiful, white blouse is not just a classic—it's sexy, too. Buy one with some Lycra, rayon, nylon or other synthetic fiber will wear better than a 100% cotton blouse, and will clean easier, and stay white longer. Make sure it fits well and is feminine. A good fit means a generous amount of fabric in the arms and at the armpits. Do the stretch test. Reach your hands around your body as if you're hugging yourself. If the blouse has enough 'give' to do this, it fits. The best part is that you can mix n match this

with trousers, skirts, jeans, etc. It gets you that formal look or suitable for a casual outing. You can have a man's shirt (white or camel) too.

7. A long sleeve tee and a short sleeve tee. The $50 tee shirt may seem like a ridiculously priced item, but there is a difference between the expensive tees and the cheap ones. The first difference is fabric. A primo tee shirt, long or short sleeved, is wonderful to touch. In fact, it invites touch, and it makes you feel sexy. Make sure the long sleeved tee is long enough in the arms. Cheaper manufacturers skimp on fabric here. V-necks are flattering if you feel you're fleshier than you'd like to be, but they don't look as good with a blazer as the scoop necks, and they don't work at all with a cardigan, so consider this when deciding scoop or V-neck. As for color, white is always great, as is black, beige, sage, baby blue or blush pink. If you're wearing your tee with more basic colors you might want to "pop" a little with some great color here.

8. A nice 'sweat suit'. NOT the kind with elastic in the ankles, but one like Juicy Couture. You'll look sexy in it, and he won't be able to keep his hands off of you. While Juicy is great, there are also lots of beautiful and well-made knock off sweat suits at Barneys, Nordstrom's and other department stores.

9. A V-neck sweater. Merino wool is a good value because it lasts a long time and wears well. Cashmere, if you can afford it. This sweater should be able to be worn alone, with a push up bra, with a tee underneath, or your camisole underneath.

I base most of my fashion taste on what doesn't itch.
—Gilda Radner

---

10. A turtleneck. Turtlenecks need to fit well. They should not be too baggy. In fact, they should not be baggy at all. Snug, but not tight, is the best fit. Choose your turtleneck in a fabric like wool, cashmere or well-woven cotton—one that will not stretch out and give so much that your own body shape is lost. The sweater should show off your figure. Make sure that the fabric of your turtleneck is not itchy on your neck. This is the one piece of clothing that is closest to your body than any other except your underwear. If the fabric does become itchy, a quick fix is a thin silky scarf that you can neatly tie around your neck on the inside of the turtleneck. The scarf should protrude just a little at the top to flash a spark of color (a hounds tooth print or paisley is nice), and should be neat, not artsy in the way it is tied and showing. Another itch tip is to avoid perfume on your neck before donning your turtleneck. Keep the spray on your wrists. Sometimes ingredients certain perfumes, mixed with the friction of a turtleneck, can

cause irritation. A nice cornstarch based powder is a good deterrent for itching. Lastly, your turtleneck should not have "cuffs" or a mock turtleneck. Cowl necks are long gone the way of culottes (remember them?). Do not try and single-handedly resurrect the cowl neck.

Extra: One big sweater. Big does not mean baggy. No cardigans, no buttons, no zippers, no ties. Just a big sweater in a wool or cotton in a thick knit with a clean lined turtle neck that is roomy, to wear with jeans, trousers, or in place of a jacket for cold climate fall or warm weather winters. A nubby, boucle, multi-colored wool sweater will work wonders. Pair this with jeans and boots or high heels. Think about wearing this on dates when you go for long walks on the beach in winter, or crisp fall walks in the park.

11. A cardigan. Choose one that you can wear or that you can tie around your neck. Make sure that this piece fits you well. Ribbed cardigans solve the baggy sweater problem. A heavy cotton knit, wool or cashmere are great, sensual fabrics for this item. A variation on this, but not a substitute for a cardigan, is the sweater coat. This is a great 'riff' on the blazer or the cardigan, and can substitute for a blazer when the occasion is less formal. This piece is also great over jeans or trousers for any weekend event or activity. And better than a poncho which will be gone as a style as fast as it arrived.

12. A coat. This year's winning comeback coat is the pea coat, and it's a chic option over anything. This coat will work with your skirt, your trousers, and your jeans. Chose camel, black or navy—even red or orange or a hounds tooth check are all nice options.

13. Pumps. Follow the same rules for pumps as you do for blue jeans. Don't acquire lots of cheap pairs of shoes. If the price was cheap, the shoes probably look cheap, and while they're great at getting you through a night out in a pinch, when you had nothing else to wear, they are not the staple you want in your closet. Buy the most expensive pair you can afford. Another variation on the pump that is also acceptable is the heeled T-strap. This classic shoe works wherever a pump does.

Extra: If your budget allows, a shearling coat is a wonderful extra for casual activities in cold weather. It's a luxurious, contemporary alternative to a mink. Choose a classic shape (jackets are fashion risks, car length coats or knee length are a best bet for style).

14. A sexy, strappy sandal. Nothing is sexier than beautiful shoes with beautiful feet. Sandals are a must have for dates and parties. Or for any occasion that you'd wear a smoky eye or extra perfume. Department stores are the easiest place to buy these because of their selection and size options. If you like patent leather, this is the time to buy it. These shoes will work well with your trousers, pencil skirt and dresses and even with jeans on certain occasions. Do not mix a strappy sandal with your Juicy sweat suit. While it's not a law, it should be. You may get a fashion police ticket from me—this is your first warning!

About half my designs are controlled fantasy, 15 percent are total madness and the rest are bread-and-butter designs.
—Manolo Blahnik

15. A sporty shoe. Many of your dates and family activities will involve tennis, hiking and other activities where you need a comfortable, supportive pair of footwear. If you have to wear flats during the day, and absolutely refuse to give them up for heels, try a driving moccasin. They're not particularly sexy, but if you have to be in the carpool lane, or are running the soccer mom gig and it's "that kind of a day" stay pretty in moccasins.

Extra: The dressier version of the moccasin is a one-inch heel backless pump, which dresses up jeans and looks very sexy. You will turn heads in the carpool lane or on the soccer mom field.

16. Boots. Leather boots in black or brown with a two-inch (or higher) heel that you can wear with trousers, jeans and skirts are killer seductress tools. Men love boots and hats on women. These are very sexy without appearing 'over the top.'

I did not have three thousand pairs of shoes. I had one thousand and sixty.
—Imelda Marcos

17. Shorts. Shorts are very sexy, but the sexiest ones are not the shortest or the tightest! In fact, make sure they are not too short. Nothing is *less* sexy to a successful and wealthy man than tramp-y looking shorts that don't fit well. Save the short and tight for the bedroom. When you're out in public, make sure your

shorts don't creep up your butt. Hot pants, like dinosaurs and Pintos, are a relic from the past. A few inches above the knee is the best length for shorts. And make sure that the fit is generous, rather than too tight. It's fine to wear a sexy top with these, but a good rule is only one sexy item per outfit. Let the top be sexy, and let the shorts be more conservative.

18. A bathing suit. The more expensive suits are made better, not just in cut, but in fabric. Gottex is a great brand for tightening up what you've got. Ralph Lauren is great for beautiful fabric. Bikinis are terrific, but G-strings and thong bikinis are risky business. Take your best friend—or whomever you know will be honest with you—along with you when you buy one of these. If you have cellulite or a big tush or a tummy that's better suited to a maillot or a boy's shorts two-piece, make sure your friend tells you. You don't want to find out your suit doesn't fit you well by overhearing strangers whispering and giggling about you, once you're at the beach or pool. If you live in warm weather climates, you'll want three or more suits in your closet because chlorine and salt water will fade the color and wear away at the elastic in and on your suit, so you'll want to rotate them.

Basic Bathing Suit Rules:
Whether you choose a one piece or two-piece, choose a swimsuit that looks best on your body. There is no age at which you cannot wear a two-piece bathing suit—just make sure that your bikini is age and body type appropriate.
* Big breasts—If you have big breasts and you want a two-piece bathing suit, try a halter shaped top that emphasizes cleavage while minimizing bounce, and providing support. The under-wire bra top will shape your bust-line by lifting and supporting to define your shape. Some bathing suits are made with built in minimizing bras.
* Generous booty—A scoop bottom will give your backside coverage so that you're not hanging out of your suit. You want a good rear view. Walk away with confidence.
* Small breasts—A push up bra top is a great look for women who want a bigger look up top. Create cleavage with under-wire support and push up pads built into the top. A padded bandeau top is also a cute look that will flatter a good figure with small breasts. Or go au natural with a triangle top—the kind that has very little support, and looks like two triangles, covering your breasts. Adjustable straps assure flexibility so you're not falling out of your top, and you can also buy these with light padding.
* Small bottoms look great in boy cut short bottoms or if you have a well-toned tummy, a string bottom flaunts your abs and everything else.

* A tankini is a great suit for small or medium sized breasts—especially if your abs are less toned than you'd like them to be. This is a flattering look with the sexy peek of tummy to let everyone know you're still wearing a two-piece.
* One-piece bathing suits are very sexy—as long as you have the right one for your body. A suit that has a diagonal print or a diagonal fabric cut is flattering to thick middles or generous tummies. A V-neck gives the illusion of more bust than you actually have and draws attention away from heavy thighs. If you have a big bust, go for a scoop or rounded neck suit.
* Get a leg up—High cut leg openings on your one-piece will give the illusion of longer legs. But if you have saddlebags or thick thighs, go for a modified leg opening. The lower cut the leg opening, the less help you get flattering your legs. If you have a boyish thin figure, a boy-cut bottom will look very sexy, whereas a high cut leg line may make you look gaunt.
* Prints or solids—A flowery or all over print hides a myriad of sins. A solid color will hide less. A bright or light solid color is only for those with terrific bodies. If you've got a great body, get a white suit—by all means! Horizontal stripes accentuate, so don't wear a horizontally striped suit if you're heavy. If you're a very thin body type, go for the stripes. Horizontal stripes on the top of a suit, will make a small bust look bigger.

Cover-ups—Do not wear a makeshift long sleeved, button down shirt as your cover up! And save the moo moos for traditional island events. Your best look for over a swimsuit is a sarong, which will never go out of style, and that you can wrap around your hips or under your arms for a sexy island cover up.

19. Sunglasses. Aside from protecting your eyes, shades put the polish on your outfit. They can also be very flirty. Go from looking great to looking really great with a good pair of sunglasses. Pick a shape that's great for your specific face, and if you're prone to losing glasses, get cheap ones. No one will know—or care.

Face shapes and the glasses shapes that are most flattering:
Oval: Any shaped frame is flattering on this happy go lucky face shape.
Round: Choose styles with high set sides, and those with color and/or decoration on the temples. Try to avoid small, round and large frames that will make your face look rounder. Avoid frames with color or decoration on the lower rim.
Heart: Choose smaller frames without decoration on the temples. You could try rounded, slender or square styles with lower sides. Try and avoid styles that are wide at the top of the frames.

Triangular: Try bold, strong and wide shapes and avoiding small, narrow frames.
Square: Round and oval style frames may help to soften the jaw line. Try to avoid
thin angular and square frames, as these will exaggerate square features.
Long: To create a balance, try wider frames with a strong top line. A large, square
frame will help to hide a long, oval frame.

20. Two handbags. One for everyday use and one for dressy affairs are basic.
Make sure that your day-to-day handbag is up to date. There is nothing that can
drag a good outfit down faster than last year's handbag. Your bag should match
most of your shoes, and be big enough to hold your palm pilot, your wallet, your
make up case and your cell phone. It should not be big enough to fit a phone
book in. Do not confuse your handbag with your kids' diaper bag, your college
backpack or your airline overnight bag. If you need more space, reconsider what
you're putting in there. You probably need a diaper bag, a backpack or an overnight bag, but for fashion, all you need is a handbag. For fancy occasions, chose a
clutch, a clutch-sized bag with a shoulder strap or a clutch with a very small handle. You can upgrade the fabric to silk, embroidered fabric or leather, or even
sparkly, and this bag should be big enough to hold a credit card, a $20 bill, a few
items of makeup and your keys.
21. A watch. Buy the most expensive one you can afford, for daytime wear. If you
can't afford a lot, don't worry. Timex makes great tank watches that cost around
$20. You can also opt for a watch with a simple black leather band, or one with a
stretchy marquisite band for an antique look.
22. Pearls. Like boobs, who cares if they're real or not? Just make sure you have
some. If you're newly purchasing your pearls, buy a strand with a length that is
close to your neck. Not hanging down your chest. This is not the 1920s. Flappers
and prohibition are not that interesting and anything too long will look costumey
instead of fashionable, making long strands too much of a fashion distraction
risk. If you already own a long strand, you can loop it around your wrist for a
four strand pearl cuff, which looks terrific.

---

*I think men who have a pierced ear are better prepared for
marriage—they've experienced pain and they've bought jewelry.*

—Rita Rudner

23. Earrings. This jewelry enhances and feminizes your face. You should wear earrings all the time. Three pairs of classics to start: one pair of studs, one pair of hoops, and one pair of dangly earrings.

A. The studs can be pearls (can't lose here), diamonds or some other gemstone. A sterling or gold, round stud is fine.

B. The hoops should be conservative in size. One or two inches is the biggest they should be, so that they're not too tribal and bohemian looking. Sterling or gold are good choices.

C. Dangly earrings are for dressing occasions. Chandelier earrings are fashionable today. This is a great style to adopt as your third pair. Another option is to go with a modified chandelier earring. Something smaller, maybe half an inch instead of a full inch or inch and a half, that only has one tier of jewels.

24. Bracelets. One simple cuff in wood, metal or any other simple natural element, with clean lines can add a dash of classic style to any outfit. A gold or silver bracelet on the same hand as your watch, in the same color tone as your watch, is also good.

But remember: Less is more. Before you leave the house for a date, look in the mirror and take off one piece of jewelry. Then you're ready to go.

Extra: If you can't live without the latest tends, the one piece of jewelry you may opt to add to your jewelry box this year is a brooch. Make it simple and only wear it on your wool blazer jacket.

---

25. Rings. If your honey has given you a ring, wear it when it matches your outfit, or wear it always to show your dedication to him. Otherwise, you can wear one ring that is the same metal as your watch/bracelet/earrings—whichever of those items you are wearing. And don't put it on your right hand, fourth finger, unless you want people to think you're taken.

26. A white camisole and a black camisole. These should have some Lycra, nylon or other fabric that clings. They should not be 100% cotton. A camisole to wear during the day should not stretch out the way cotton does. You want this to look crisp and inviting. Do not wear this camisole as a substitute for lingerie when you're out and about. Wear this over your bra, but under your V-neck sweater or V-neck tee shirt.

27. Bras. A good push up bra, a good everyday bra and a good sports bra are your basics. The right bra will leave you free to forget your breasts, so he can think about them!

*Unless you have prohibitively large breasts, a good push up bra is flattering, fun and a great enhancer for your wardrobe. A push up bra can change the look of your clothes and make demure look sexy at the same time—which is perfect for dating. Try one with a water or silicone cup as well as traditional padded push-ups. Buy one in white and one in black.

*An everyday bra that has a smooth cup is essential for a clean line under tee shirts, sweaters and dresses.

* And a supportive and fashionable sports bra for tennis, hiking, yoga practice, spinning class and other sporty dates and activities is a must.

In addition to the basics, build a wardrobe of sexy bras for play and fun, especially those that come with matching panties. He'll love you in these.

28. Panties. Please don't commit lingerie suicide! Women who wear raggedy underwear under $400 dresses are undermining the whole effect. Besides the fact that, as my mother always said, "Make sure your undergarments are clean and have no holes in them, you never know when you may have an accident."

Don't underestimate the value of your mental attitude when you know you look well from the skin up-or from having the absolutely right foundation under your dress, AND men notice lingerie! Your panties and bra should match and they should always look 'inviting'! Do not skimp on your lingerie…Trust me on this one! Panty-wear is extremely important—and not just because of what it covers. You don't want to be seen with panty lines. You don't want bunching underwear to ruin the look of your clothes. You don't want elastic that is frayed for when your clothes come off. You don't want anything that is too big or too small. You want panties that look good with your clothes or without your clothes.

Extras: Pinks, ice blue, lemon and tangerine are fun colors for lingerie, and any color that makes you feel lighthearted and fun is perfect for weekend wear when the mood is casual. For sexy occasions, boy's shorts-panties with matching bras and other matching sets are great, as are those adorable matching camisole and panty sets. But these are strictly for indoor fun.

Here's a way to start your panty collection: Good bikini underwear is a basic, as is a G-string, if you're comfortable in it. Try out a thong and a G-string to see what is more comfortable for you. Although they are guilty of being the butt of all butt floss jokes, G-strings are also the antidotes to panty lines and the next best thing to going commando. G-strings are also surprisingly comfortable. If you're experimenting, grab a cheap Victoria's Secret or Frederick's of Hollywood G-string and thong and see which works better for you. They are terrific for your Juicy sweat suit or any clothing that offers a view of your butt. You want a sleek form fitting shape and line. Make sure you have classic whites in your panty/bra wardrobe as well as classic black.

"I like my clothes to be tight enough to show I'm a woman, but loose enough to show I'm a lady."

—Mae West

---

29. Scarves—Keep and build a collection of scarves that range from silk to mohair to cashmere to bandanas, so that you have them for all occasions, and can just grab one from your scarf drawer.

30. Belts—Make sure that you have a nice collection of belts that coordinate with all your clothes. The width of the belt should both match the loopholes in your trousers or skirt, and should also be a fashionable width. Keep a black leather belt, a brown leather belt and a metallic belt as staples. Add anything else you find that's interesting to your stash.

An extra don't: Pantyhose
Pantyhose are just not sexy. And don't even think about wearing stockings (or pantyhose, for that matter) with sandals. Do wear thigh highs and stockings whenever possible.

Before you leave the house (or let anyone in)

1) Refuse to wear anything too tight, too cheap, too clingy, or that makes you want to blush.

2) There is nothing less sexy or less chic than tugging at things.

3) What looks great at a party is often better covered up on the street and subway and no, you are not being a prude—just prudent.

4) Things that are meant to be sexy just look trashy if the cut is too skimpy.

5) Too tight as opposed to snuggly sleek—is the kiss of death for anyone aspiring to be chic.

Remember these Rules of the Closet:

1. Never wear dirty clothes. If you spill red wine or an item of clothing, and are able to rinse it in club soda or cold water and salt, do so immediately. If you can't attend to the stain immediately, take the clothes to the dry cleaners as soon as

possible. You may not wear clothes with stains on them. Sorry. It looks like you don't care about your clothes, your appearance, and ultimately other things. Whether or not it's true that is the impression dirty clothes telegraph.

2. Wrinkled clothing is not acceptable. Have your clothes professionally pressed or iron them yourself. Again, they project the impression that you don't care. A quick fix for wrinkles is a steamy, hot shower—not for you, for your clothes. If your clothes are wrinkled and you're in a pinch, turn your shower on as hot as it will go, leave the shower door open, and hang your item of clothing in the bathroom, far enough away from the open shower door so that it won't get wet, but close enough so that it will get steamed. Shut the bathroom door and leave your clothing in the steamy bathroom with the hot shower running for as long as you can, or as long as the hot water holds out. This will steam wrinkles out.

3. Maintain your wardrobe. Fix holes. Fix hems that un-raveled. If clothes are worn at the knees or the butt, give them to Goodwill. Spend one hour a month doing maintenance on your wardrobe. Treat it the same way you would a garden—with care.

Color factoids:
<u>Green</u>
* Green is thought to be the color chosen for U.S. currency because it represents strength and stability.
*Research conducted at Washington State University and published in the journal Horttechology (yes, this is the correct spelling) suggests that people in rooms with a lot of greenery can tolerate more physical pain that those in surroundings without any plants.
*In Celtic myths green was associated with fertility.
*In the 15th century, the color green was the best choice for a bride's gown because of its earliest symbolism.
*Of note is the continued symbolism attached to the color green in the latter part of this century. Urban mythology says that anyone who chooses a green M&M is sending a somewhat similar message. Green has been reinterpreted by late 20th century American culture to signify a state of heightened sexuality in this specific situation.
*Ancient Egyptians felt that green was a sacred color representing the hope and joy of spring.
*Green is a sacred color to Moslems.
*Suicides dropped 34% when London's Black Friar Bridge was painted green.
*Currently the most popular decorating color, green symbolizes nature.
*It is a calming, refreshing color. People waiting to appear on TV sit in "green rooms" to relax
* Dark green is masculine, conservative, and implies wealth.

<u>White</u>
*White is the color of virginity in America.
*White is an inappropriate color for a wedding in China. It is the color of mourning there.
* Doctors and nurses wear white to imply sterility.

<u>Red, white and blue</u>:
*Although there is no official record of the meaning of the colors of the U.S. flag, in 1782, the Congress of the Confederation chose these same colors for the Great Seal of the United States and listed their meaning as follows: white to mean purity and innocence, red for valor and hardiness, and blue for vigilance, perseverance, and justice.

Black
*The color of authority and power—but black can also imply submission. Priests wear black to signify submission to God. Some fashion experts say a woman wearing black implies submission to men.
*Villains often wear black.

Red
*Red is stimulating and exciting.
*Red clothing gets noticed.
*Red cars are popular targets for thieves. As a general rule red cars cost more to insure than other color cars.
*Red is the color of love.

Pink
*Pink is romantic and tranquilizing.
*Sports teams sometimes paint the locker rooms used by opposing teams bright pink so their opponents will lose energy.

Blue
*Blue is peaceful and causes the body to produce calming chemicals, so it is often used in bedrooms.
*Fashion consultants recommend wearing blue to job interviews because it symbolizes loyalty.
*People are more productive in blue rooms. Studies show weightlifters are able to handle heavier weights in blue gyms.

Yellow
Bright yellow gets attention.
*People lose their tempers more often in yellow rooms, and babies will cry more if their nursery is yellow.
*Yellow enhances concentration, hence its use for legal pads.
*Yellow also speeds metabolism.

Purple
*Purple is associate with royalty, luxury, wealth, and sophistication.

Brown
*Light brown implies genuineness.
*Men are more apt to say brown is one of their favorite colors.

13

There's No Place Like Home

◆

There's No Place Like Home,
There's No Place Like Home...

Men love cozy nests with all the creature comforts possible. You want him to want to spend time with you, at your home, so make sure you have a well feathered nest that is inviting, cozy and luxurious, and makes him want to stay and come back again and again.

First, some absolute musts
Your place must...
• Be clean—Vacuumed, dusted, and smelling fresh
• Be lit dimly—Soft mood lighting can add a lot to a room, regardless of the condition of the rest of its furnishings
• Be free of "Other Guy" evidence
• Not be a warehouse, dorm, or office—A cluttered, unorganized home says you have a cluttered, unorganized life
• Be free of pets and their...accidents—If Rover has made an accident on the carpet, please, for the love of God, clean it up before we get there. Use baking soda to quickly eliminate the stain and the odor, just sprinkle, let dry, then vacuum. If you have a litter box somewhere in your place, make sure that is clean and that the house doesn't smell like you have cats. He shouldn't know you have them before he actually sees them.

Seduction 101
Creating a romantic environment will put him 'in the mood.'

Music—Barry White, Sade, Julio and Enrique Iglesias, and Maxwell are a good start to your collection.

Candlelight—Candlelight makes everyone look great while instantly creating a romantic mood. If you don't have any, pick up some votive candles; they're quick, easy, and inexpensive.

Healthy Plants—Lush plants immediately make a house feel warmer, happier, and homier:

• If you buy flowers make your first purchase some easy to care for plants like orchids.
• Philodendrons are what I call "no-kill" plants, and make a great choice if you don't have a green thumb.
• Bamboo, used in Feng Shui and very popular, is great for a casual area, and requires almost no maintenance.

Feng Shui—an ancient system that teaches you where to put things in your home (like those flowers you just bought). Feng shui is designed to ward off evil spirits while welcoming good ones (like the looove spirit). This is a GREAT conversation starter.

Wine, champagne and chocolates—Chocolates (like oysters) are said to be an aphrodisiac and when you want to create a romantic evening at home and impress that special man with your attention to every detail, consider:

• A plate full of bittersweet chocolates, with a beautiful flower garnish and a snifter of Disaronno Amaretto liqueur
• A couple Kir Royals (Champagne with a splash of Chambord) and a plate of white chocolates and raspberries.

No Distractions—Answering machine on. Volume off. Better yet get voicemail.
Clean towels—No explanation needed.
Clean sheets and pillowcases—Ditto.

An impeccable bathroom—Have plenty of toilet paper, stash all feminine hygiene products, and put the toilet seat d-o-w-n., and a medicine cabinet with nothing to make him squirm over (just assume he'll be taking a snoop while he's in there).

- A painting or picture in the bathroom works wonders.
- Dog-eared "Bride" and "Wedding" magazines, on the other hand, do not.

> Factoid: Foods that are perfectly okay to eat with your fingers include: artichokes, bacon, french fries, sandwiches and small fruits and berries.

Create a comfy, classy
If you shop around at garage sales or flea markets, you can get some of the best-made furnishings around for a steal.

Lamps and Shades—Purchase a variety of lamps and lampshades of different styles and heights. Mixing and matching will create a customized look (designers do this all the time.)

Cheap and Chic Art—If you don't have original art and can't afford to buy it, head to your local art museum and hit the gift shop where you'll find various posters and prints of all sizes. Next, pick up some simple ready-made frames, insert the poster or print, and hang. You will be amazed at the differences it makes! And if you're really in a pinch, some main branch libraries will let you borrow art that is already framed. You can just hang it at home.

Small space savvy

Mirrors—Mirrors give the illusion of space and add depth to a room. Place a large mirror opposite a window for a fabulous result.

If you cannot afford to have mirrors professionally installed try square mirror tiles that can be purchased inexpensively at your local home supply store. They come with a sticky adhesive on the back so all you have to do is position the mirror tile into place.

Paint—Color not only sets the decorative style, but influences perception of size and space. It can literally transform a room, providing the biggest bang for your buck and your time.

White paint on the ceiling is the best. It will help to reflect light and the lighter the room appears, the larger it will appear.

Monochromatic Colors—A small place can be made to flow and look bigger by using the same colors throughout.

Blues and greens will make a room appear larger and airier.

The reverse is true of reds, yellows and oranges, which make a room cozier and more intimate.

Dark colors will make a room look smaller, and can actually make it feel as if the walls are coming in on you.

Four furniture fyis
1. Avoid large, bulky scaled furniture in small rooms.
2. Upholstered furniture with low backs and arms will appear less obtrusive.
3. Consider open legged chairs, glass coffee table tops instead of solid wood ones.
4. A love seat may work better than a full sized sofa. Equally two chairs may work better than a love seat in combination with a large sofa.

A quickie living room face lift
Focal Point—Create a "focal point" by focusing attention to one area of the room. The simplest way to create a focal point is to place your sofa on the longest wall of the room. Then hang a large painting or framed mirror above the sofa.

In the newly created "focal point," create a conversation space. A U-shaped conversation area is ideal and can easily be accomplished by placing a matching pair of chairs or is seated to face everyone else.

Groupings—Next, group any remaining furniture or other items into pairs.

Slipcovers—Consider investing in some ivory (off-white) slipcovers. Ivory matches everything and slipcovers have evolved to the point where they now offer lots of attractive options at a very reasonable price. To the slipcovers, add a few large-scale pillows that are the same color of the slipcovers, but in a different pattern or texture.

Pillows—If you cannot afford slipcovers, then simply buy some large-scale ivory pillows for your sofa (or another solid, neutral color that matches the sofa's fabric) along with a large throw (in the same color) and place it over the back of the couch.

In the kitchen where things really heat
Tiles—Damaged, stained or missing tiles? Don't panic. Move your dishwasher, stove or refrigerator instead! If you don't tell, no one will ever know they are missing! It'll just be our little secret.

Cabinets and Walls—Repaint those cabinets, guys! It'll make a world of difference. If you have wood cabinets, repaint the walls with some color. It will make the wood appear richer, and emphasize your accessories.

Glass = Class—Ladies, no plastic glasses. No matter how cute you think they are. If you don't have glasses or stemware to serve cocktails or after dinner drinks in…get some. The difference in the presentation and a man's perception of you will be well worth the small investment.

The bedroom, where it all goes
Sheets—I said it before, but it bears repeating; dirty sheets are not an option. It's also worth it to make an investment in soft sheets. How do you know soft sheets from rough ones? Well, if your hands can't tell, let the thread-count guide your way. The higher the count, the better to, ahem…lay down on.

Bedroom Windows—If you have neighbors, you're going to need window treatments in your bedroom. My suggestion, if you are on a budget, is to invest in sheer vertical blinds. They are simple, clean, and will add height to your window. Best of all, they're reasonably priced.

The Five Senses—Work 'em. Men are creatures of comfort. They are visual and sensual. So keep this in mind when working on your love nest. They want soft sheets to touch. They want smooth music to listen to. A light scented candle to smell. They want something beautiful to look at (flowers will do). And yes, a few treats to tantalize his taste buds would be the cherry on top.

One last tip: seal and peel
Drafts can be a real problem in the winter and buying new windows can be costly. So what do you do if you can't afford to replace your windows and realize that plastic covering isn't going to impress anyone? Use caulk. That's right. Caulk around the windows in the winter and then, literally, peel it off in the summer so that you can open the windows. It's inexpensive, it's easy, and it solves the problem effectively.

Top 10 Quick and Easy Man Magnets For Your Home
If you want your home to be "Man-Ready," stock up on these things men love. He'll never want to leave your house.
* Meat—keep a couple of steaks in the freezer just in case, and a bottle of good red wine in the cabinet.
* Sex—condoms, ladies, and clean, fluffy towels for showers afterwards.
* Great bodies—go to the gym and the salon.
* Big televisions—bigger is better, remember?
* Cars—every cliché applies. Get a great car. It can be an expensive sports car or a classic. You'll have another source of man magnet in the Valet Parking lane. He'll have to wonder who's got that hot car—and when it turns out to be a hot woman....
* Sports—make sure your cable TV menu receives ESPN, ESPN, Fox Sports Net, Fox Sports Net 2
* Dogs—don't necessarily get one, but love his. Buy it toys.
* Being cared for and waited on—in every way
* Dessert—chocolate mousse is easy to make. Or keep a cheesecake in the freezer.
* The Sports Section—from your local newspaper and The Business Section from The Wall Street Journal

Section III:
The Bedroom

The art of sex is sadly left to racy television shows and books to teach us what to do, when really, this information is a gift that should be passed down from loved one to loved one through the generations. But hopefully, you'll think of me as your family of sorts, and allow me to tell you what it is that men like, so that you can keep him coming back to you again and again.

You've probably heard the cliche that men want a lady and a whore (in one) in the bedroom. Well, it's true. They do. But it's not really a whore they want so much as someone who is comfortable with sex. Giving pleasure and receiving pleasure, sexually, is one of life's reasons for being, and when your lover or boyfriend or husband takes you to bed, what happens there is the only thing in this busy world that is truly between the two of you. So, make it count. Make what happens in the bedroom so delectable, that he can't get what you two have done together—or you—out of his mind.

Which is where you need to start. For god's sakes turn off the telephone, the television and focus all your attention on him. Everything you have done up until now—making a good first impression, dating and preening for dating, conversing and flirting—it all culminates here, in bed. This is why he is dating—for sex with a woman he loves or wants to love. And this is why you have engaged and enticed him, to allow him to win your affections.

Everything he does in the bedroom is right. Every part of his body is good. And everything you do together is as it should be. This is not the time or place to be squeamish or prudish. This is a place where you must never let boredom set its head to rest. This is a playground—for adults. You must keep him engaged time and again, and that means you must keep your body, your grooming, your lingerie and bed clothes, and your interests and education here, as current as you do in public, social situations. If it sounds like a lot of work, relax. The reason you keep your sexual self as well maintained as your working self, or your family self is so that you can have the same confidence and allure in the bedroom that you have at a party or a dance.

Once here, let his mood guide you, as you give him pleasure—and absolutely let him give you pleasure, too. Explore his body with a mixture of sophistication and newfound awe. Bring your expertise to the bedroom, but allow for surprises—for his body is unique, and while all men have pretty much the same parts, each human being responds differently to each touch.

What happens here, in the bedroom, is really a barometer for the rest of the relationship. If the sex is good, there is a margin for error and compatibility everywhere else. If the sex is not good, or if it's not happening, everything else that is petty will take on greater proportions. So take it upon yourself to make sure that the sex is good—for both of you. And that means allowing him to conquer you and give you pleasure that only he can give, so that he feels you will keep coming back to him, as well as he will be wanting you when he is not with you, and hoping the next time you two are together is sooner rather than later.

14

Sex: Coming Together Between The Sheets

Ann Landers said that you are addicted to sex if you have sex more than 3 times a day, and that you should seek professional help. I have news for Ann Landers: The only way I am going to get sex 3 times a day is if I seek professional help.
—Jay Leno

By now you know that men and women are different—really different. But perhaps there is no area of your romantic life where that is more evidence than in the bedroom. Understanding how your man thinks about sex can save you countless hours of pain, of obsession and can even save your relationship. Because this part of your relationship can be the most gratifying, it can also be fraught with the most danger. It's up to you to decide if sex is going to be something that brings you together, or drives you apart.

I see it over and over: Young relationships that are on a smooth sailing course until sex is introduced. Then, even the smartest and savviest women can get their buttons pushed in a way that makes them crazy and threatens the whole relationship. The number one reason why? Sex means something different to women and men. And women who don't understand and appreciate this difference will drive their man away. Don't let this happen to you.

Timing is everything. Well, sort of…
Lets start at the beginning. You've done the work that we've been discussing so far: you've gotten really specific about what you want in a man. You've gone to a target rich area. You've met a great guy and you've let him pursue you. You're in a relationship. The first question is when should you have sex? While there is no mathematical formula, there are a few guidelines. The first one is, obviously, not too soon. What do I mean by not too soon? At the very least, don't sleep with him on the first three dates.

In three dates you will let this guy pursue you, you will let him wine and dine you, and you'll let him know he's found a prize...a woman worth wooing. The ultimate trophy for his valiant efforts is sex with you, of course. So what happens if you give him sex too early? He doesn't feel like you are a real prize, and if you're not a real prize then he's not a winner, and he needs to feel like a winner.

Think of it this way.... You train for a marathon, you complete the race, you stand on the podium and you receive a trophy. You will treasure that trophy forever. Compare that with someone just handing you the same trophy for no work. It's meaningless. Sorry, ladies, that's just how it is—that's how men think. I'm not saying you can't go out and have sex with men on the first date. Do it all you like, as long as you're being safe. I'm saying don't do it with a guy you're interested in having a long-term relationship with.

Here's something else that might surprise you: While you shouldn't have sex too soon, you shouldn't wait too long either. There is a time when it will just come naturally, to both of you. While it comes naturally to men 24 hours a day, if you listen to your body, you will know you are ready for it too. That happens for most women from three weeks to a month. And if you go on too long without it, it can create an awkward and artificial atmosphere in the relationship. You don't want to be "just friends" with this man, so don't act like he's just a friend. A friend of mine who is a successful producer was in a flirtatious relationship with an A-list director. She was reading "The Rules" at the time—and took its advice. What happened? The two-month mark in the relationship came and went. She thought she was making him "hot" by making him wait, but she pushed that rule past its "natural" course, and the relationship never recovered. He moved on.

Unlike most other dating experts, I don't feel women should hold back from having sex simply because of any so-called 'rules of dating.' That's not to imply that everyone should rush into a sex on the first date.... However, the truth is, a man is much more likely to commit to a relationship if it includes sex. Moreover, men go through life hoping and praying to one day meet that elusive beautiful and sexy woman who just can't keep her hands off him.

The bottom-line? While playing standoffish and cool may work with a few, generally speaking, if you make a man feel good about himself, sexually, he'll feel great about you and excited about being with you. He'll want to be with you—and making him want is what you want.

Remember, if you smoke after sex, you're doing it too fast.
                                                    —Woody Allen

Setting the Stage

Just because you are not having sex right away doesn't mean you should not be sexual. On the contrary: The first step in your sexual relationship? Those first smoldering glances, the good night kisses and "make out" sessions. In those first several dates, while you are finding out who your guy is, you can and must still be sexual, even if you are not actually having sex. In fact, cultivating your sexuality does not mean buying crotch-less panties by the dozen. It means thinking of yourself, and feeling that you are sexual whether or not you are having sex.

What does this mean? Well, you will dress in a way that is sexually pleasing to him and in turn makes you feel more sexual. Your eyes will show him a glimpse of the sexual imp you have inside. Your look and your glance, the way you move your eyes over him—are sexual tools. Without a vulgar word, you can imply a myriad of sexual interests with your look. Your eyes are important—not just as windows into your soul—but windows into your sexual self. In fact when someone is sexually interested in you, his pupils will dilate, as will yours, when you are interested in him. Think of it, between us, as his optical erection!

Then there is your touch. Not groping, and not stroking like a high school heavy petting session in the back seat of a car after a football game, but as a cultivated, sexual woman, who knows that the lightest touch can imply the greatest yield. There are many ways to touch him without holding hands (don't you dare hold his hand first!) or putting your arms around each other. When you brush a lock of his hair out of his eyes, be conscious of the sensation of that millisecond your fingertips touch his forehead. If you are aware of it, trust me, he will see that sensuality in your eyes, and it will get him hot. When you eat dinner with him, although you are across the table in a crowded restaurant, the way you touch your wineglass stem is sexually suggestive of how you will touch him—if he is lucky enough to win you.

When you kiss, forget about pecks on the cheek. You will give and receive kisses that are deep and intimate. Intimacy, however, is not measured by how far you each get your tongues down the others' throat. Lips, teeth, and every inch of the mouth and face are your playground when you're not having sex. Men think of sex in terms of orifices. Allow him to see how much pleasure and desire you can create on just his face. In fact, kissing is how many men and women gauge how the actual sex will be before they have it. Even though you are making him wait for sex, through kissing and "making out" you will be showing your guy that you are sexual, you are interested, and it will be well worth his wait—in fact this is why he will wait. You'll be driving him crazy with desire, yet holding back the big prize, sex. You will tell him, without words, that you are a sexy and sexual woman and you are so worth wanting—and waiting for.

> *It is not true that sex degrades women—if it is any good.*
> —Alan Partridge

And what are you waiting for? Well, you're waiting to get all the signals that this is a guy you want to be in a relationship with. He is caring, he is considerate, he is responsible, and he fits that "short list" of traits that you are looking for. You also want to feel out, in the most casual way possible, that he wants what you want, which is a long-term relationship, a marriage, children, what have you. Not necessarily that he wants that all this very second, with you, but that he is not opposed to it and you're both on a similar time frame. This is not accomplished through interrogating him, but through casual conversation. Definitely not, "Where do you see this going? Do you want to marry soon?" But simply and casually: "What are your goals for the future?" "Where do you see yourself in five years?" A man who wants a relationship won't be afraid to tell you.

What you don't want is to use sex to get the answers to these questions. You want to know the answers to them before you get in the bedroom. Because like it or not, sex chemically "hooks" a woman more than a man. So it is your job to be responsible enough to know this is a man you want to be hooked to. And if you know you've found a man that you want to be hooked to, sex is where you hook him back.

When the Dating Game becomes the Mating Game, don't confuse the issue! So you've found a great guy, you've felt him out, you enjoy each other and you are generally looking for the same things in a relationship. Great. Now to the fun part: Sex. As we said before, this can be a fantastic new part of the relationship, one that drives it forward and gives you both pleasure, or it can be the thing that sinks it. It truly is your choice. How do you make it work for you? You make it work by understanding why it is that men have sex, and why it is that women have sex—and the very different reasons they each have it.

Men are hard wired to need a sexually physical release, first and foremost. Emotional intimacy comes second. I repeat: for men, sex is first and foremost a hard wired physical need. That is just the way they are. Women are just the opposite. We're looking for an emotional connection first, and the physical pleasure is just a by-product. If you consider our biology it isn't that surprising. To have sex with a man, we have to allow our body to be "invaded" in a way. We need to trust a man before we let him do that.

> *Anybody who believes that the way to a man's heart is through his stomach, flunked geography.*
>
> —Robert Byrne

So here is the problem. He wants sex. You want emotional intimacy. A woman's mistake is to have a sexual relationship with a man, and put her first need, emotional intimacy, first, and to place the man's first need, a great physical release, second, sometimes even making it conditional on having sex. You are going to insist that you get what you want in exactly the way you want it, or he won't get what he wants. This creates a power struggle, and as you know, it is important for men to win all battles. So that's a bad situation. Another bad scenario is that you will pretend that he wants what you want, and be hurt when that doesn't turn out to be the case. After reading this book this far, you are way to wise to do that any more. You know he doesn't want what you want, and expecting that leads to no end of confusion and heartache. Start begging for emotional reassurances before, during and after, and you will confuse the whole issue and even introduce guilt into sex. Ladies, you can get intimacy lots of places, and in lots of ways, but sex is sex. So think like a man. They need the physical release first. They don't want to talk after sex, they don't necessarily want to snuggle after sex, they don't want to bond, and they don't want to be asked what they're feeling or what they're thinking. DON'T TAKE IT PERSONALLY! It doesn't mean he's not into you. It's just the way he's hard wired. Demand or expect something other than that and you're going to make the man feel like he is doing something wrong, when he is simply being how he was born to be. Make sex about sex. Make intimacy about intimacy. When you have sex to take care of your primary need and not his, neither of your needs will get met. When you have sex to take care of his primary need first, both of your needs will get met. If you do everything I've told you so far, a.) You two will both have great sex; and that will, b.) Eventually, the sex will lead to greater intimacy, and c.) You'll both have a whole lot more fun in the process. If you don't, you will end up stressed out, with nothing to show for it.

What do I mean by making sex a great physical act? Don't think and don't over-analyze when you're in bed. Men want sex. They love sex. But what is the difference between good and great sex for a man? The difference is your pleasure. Men love giving a woman pleasure, making her happy, seeing she's sexually satisfied. It is a huge turn on for them. So give them that, and what you get in return is obvious…no end to your own pleasure, and the kind of amazing bonding that will create true intimacy.

Sex is not the answer. Sex is the question. Yes is the answer.
—Swami X

Many women will blow a gasket when they read the words, "take the meaning out of it." I'm not saying that sex is meaningless, I am saying you should find the meaning in the relationship before you even get into bed with him (and if there is no meaning, don't have sex with him). Women look for sex to create the meaning, and that is totally backward. If you've vetted this guy, if you think he has what you are looking for, and you are ready to have sex, dive in with gusto and without reservation. You already have the meaning, now dive into great sex. Allow your most primal sexual self to emerge. He wants that.

Don't worry that you are too fat. Let go of all childish sexual guilt. Don't worry that you are not doing it right. Don't worry about anything. He wants to be in bed with a sexual woman—not a worrywart. Your only job right now is to love your body, love his body, and love the sex, and make sure he knows it.

Express Yourself

How do you make sure he knows it? First by telling him. Communicate. Tell him how good everything he does makes you feel. Be specific. If there's something he's doing that you really like a lot, let him know. If you'd rather he do that thing he just did a minute ago instead of this thing he's doing now, tell him. He wants to be good. Men cannot get praised enough, especially in this area. Everything from, "Your kisses make me melt!" to "You're driving me so crazy." Then stop talking. Don't be afraid to whimper and moan. Allow your body to actually work without your inhibiting it. Be aware and learn how your body works sexually, and how his does, too. The more you let go, the more you'll get.

If you are at all inhibited about a man's body, the blowjob is probably the most daunting act because it takes some skill. But that is why a great BJ is a woman's best weapon to hook a man. Men love the sensation and they love the visual and psychological benefits they derive from this act. They also experience vulnerability, with you in this act that they don't experience in any other part of their lives as hunters and successful businessmen. Having his most valued possession in your total control is very intimate for a man. If you show him not just a good time and a pleasurable sensation, but expertise and sophistication here, he will forever be in your power.

For many women it is an acquired taste, so to speak. But frankly, aren't all the finer things in life? Coffee, wine, and oysters—you probably gagged at all of these things once upon a time, and now you relish them. In fact, if you are prone to gagging, pay attention when you "imbibe." Try to position your body and his to lessen any gagging. The gag reflex is a physical function. If you can avoid—or go gingerly around—this part of your anatomy, with his, you won't gag. You may also want to try bypassing that part of your throat by taking in more rather than less. The trick is to experiment, and he will be willing, trust me.

A great blowjob is not brain surgery. All you have to do is think to yourself, if I had this thing, what would feel good to me? You don't like being roughly attacked at first, and neither do men. Soft and slow to start will drive him wild. The underside is more sensitive than the topside. If you don't like the taste at first (and all men, like all women, taste different), "sample it." Your own saliva will dilute any taste you don't like, and will lubricate to enhance his pleasure. Swallowing or not is strictly up to you. Use your hands all you want…you don't have to "deep throat" like in the movies. And let him know you're enjoying it! Ask him if he likes certain things, and take his direction. Tell him you want to know exactly how to please him. Believe me, he will be more than happy to let you know!

Ditto for receiving oral sex. Remember, men want to please you. This can be an equally vulnerable position for you, the same way it is for men receiving oral sex. Relax and get used to it. Tell him exactly what you want, in an encouraging way. "When you lick me soft it makes me crazy!" "I love it when you do that to me." You don't have to fake pleasure, you deserve it, girlfriend! When you are both truly having great sex, you both know it...and that can create a foundation for your whole relationship.

> *The penis mighter than the sword.*
>
> —Mark Twain

When you're happy, he's happy

It's a scientific fact: men are visual creatures. They will want to watch you go down on them, and they will go wild when they see you are into it. Another way to appeal to their visual side is lingerie. Always wear the sexy matching bra and panties. It drives them wild and makes you feel like a sex goddess too. This is also a great way to keep thinks interesting, exciting and different. Women spend far more time picking out a designer handbag than their lingerie, and a man won't even remember you OWN a handbag let alone whether it's Prada, Louis Vuitton or whatever, but he will remember the lingerie. Don't skimp here. Show him he's special and worth dressing for.

The most important thing to men about women is sex, and therefore, if he thinks he's not good at this, he may think you're the reason he's not good at it. Whether or not he's right, that's how he's thinking. You cannot underestimate how important sex is to men, and on the flip side, how insecure and vulnerable men are when it comes to sex. Therefore, it's important to them that you are enjoying sex because it translates to them that they are good at it. When it is over, if you start demanding reassurances of his feelings, his motives, his love...in short, if you start demanding that your emotional needs get met right here right now, it will make him feel trapped and insecure. It will make him feel that you were only into the sex to get this "prize" you are now demanding, and not because he was any good at it. Remember, your pleasure is his biggest prize.

Don't force your man to be a woman!

When it is all over, men will be exhausted because sex is more of a physical act for them. Some men like to talk and cuddle after sex, but many more don't. Don't take it personally. Men don't show intimacy by talking. They show it in doing for you, in tiny little ways like making you coffee in the morning. Learn to see these little things as a mans way of saying, "I care for you." When you're both having great sex, where you are both enjoying it without conditions, it will build trust, it will start breaking down barriers. Soon, you will see increased intimacy in little ways…he will put his hand on your hip while sleeping, he will want to spoon with you in the morning.

For those of you who are saying, "But why can't they be more like us!" all I can tell you is this: One day you will find yourself in a relationship with a feminine man, who likes to discuss his feelings, who likes to shop, who talks baby talk in bed and is always wondering if you love him enough. He's the guy that calls you twice a day, who pouts when you don't call right back, and who soon enough…. you will want dead. As much as we say we want men to be like us, we really don't. It's great to be different. It's great to learn how to compliment each other. It's great to learn things from each other. And one huge thing we can learn from men is how to love sex for sex. Do that and watch your whole relationship blossom.

Funny factoid: Using a feather is kinky. Using the whole chicken is perverted.

A Beginner's Guide to Kinky Sex Play

Okay. You're not a tramp, but you like sex, and you know there's more out there than what's been in your repertoire, and life is short, and you want to have some fun, so...relax. Take your time, and introduce these elements into the bedroom. Your creativity and his—are the only limits you have.

* Ice—A simple glass of ice cubes. Start with the sensual and see where it takes you. Embarrassed that you don't know what you're doing? Don't be. Experiment. Swap the ice cube from mouth to mouth in your kisses. Run it over his body, and let him run it over yours. Before you know it, everything will have melted.

* A silk scarf—You don't have to be the dominatrix or bondage master to have a little fun with silk in bed. As long as you're both consenting adults, you can see what it's like to use the scarf as a sensual texture, a blindfold or a restraint.

* A feather—The pure pleasure of a sensation on your skin...

* The floor—Sounds simple, but the bed and the sofa are tried and true make out geography. Try some new turf.

Now. You've passed Kink 101. Intermediate class is on your time!

15

Now The Challenge: Keep The Flame Alive

♦

Keep Him Wanting More!

The love you take it equal to love you make.
—The Beatles

We have our eyes on the prize for so long, we let out a big sigh of relief when we think we've found it. Sometimes we let out a long sigh. You've been looking and hoping for so long, you might feel like letting your guard down just a tiny bit, now that you think you've Finally Found Him.

After all, you've been dating three months, six months, or a year or more, and all is going smoothly. Your single girlfriends are looking at you with sweet envy. This was the way you've always dreamed it would be. It's become practically effortless. You've met his friends, you've met his parents...it's only a matter of time before you have a ring on your finger, and you can totally relax! Right? Wrong.

Let me rub this into your brains: you must always PRESERVE YOUR RELA-TIONSHIP with your man. If you are dating someone special, that work is never over. If the dating is going well, you are creating the building blocks that will support your relationship for a lifetime. And, if the dating is going well, you also have a real bond with this person, intellectually, emotionally and physically. You should maintain all of these parts, so that the same spark that that first brought the two of you together is always ablaze! A little effort each day keeps you going a long way.

Eighty percent of married men cheat in America.
The rest cheat in Europe.

Be aware of why relationships fail

All relationships are vulnerable at any time—even marriages. The current adultery statistics show that 60 percent of men cheat on their wives and 40 percent of women cheat on their husbands.

I have not failed. I've just found 10,000 ways that don't work.
—Thomas Alva Edison

Different people cheat for different reasons. For example, a couple grows apart and forgets (or not made the effort) to communicate and connect both emotionally and physically; the relationship settles into a routine—or a rut; one (or both) of the partners starts to think that maybe someone else can give them the same feelings that their spouse once did. The sad fact is no relationship is totally secure. I'm not saying this to send you into a panicked frenzy. I'm just telling you this so that you can conduct your relationship in a way that incorporates the best defense: a good offense.

If you're in a newly committed relationship, you shouldn't be worrying about whether or not you're man is likely to cheat on you, but there are certain measures you can take to make him happier and therefore, lessen the likelihood that he'd go looking somewhere else. Yes, this man is in a relationship with you, and at this point only you, but it is important to keep him attracted to you—and wanting you. Complacency can make cold fish out of even the hottest couple. Stay interested and interesting—gone may be the days of courtship, but the seduction should never stop.

Sex alleviates the tension caused by love.
—Anonymous

Tips for keeping love alive!
1. Take good care of yourself. Let's be honest. Your man is more likely to stray if you've let yourself go. And if that alone is not enough reason to keep good look-

ing, consider that studies have proven that when we look good, we tend to feel good. So do it for him and for you.

2. Communicate. Don't just talk, listen, and hear. Interestingly, many people do not stray for s-e-x, rather they stray because they're looking for someone who listens to them, who 'understands them,' and who believes in them. If something is not right between you two, talk openly about it—immediately. Don't allow time for things to fester and grow. And not just about problems—communicate about hopes and dreams, and what you want to do next—whether it's take a vacation, build a new house or try a new sexual position!

3. Show admiration and respect for your guy. Everyone likes to feel appreciated, and men need to feel good about themselves, especially from the woman in their life. Always express your interest in what's he's doing. Men have fragile egos and your interest will make him feel validated and that what he's doing is important—to you. It will also give him the confidence he needs to continue going out in the world each day and conquer dragons.

4. Spend quality time together doing things you both enjoy. While it's great to establish some "dating traditions," don't let your dating get into a rut. Go to new places. Try new activities.

5. Keep the "x" in your sex life. While at first your sex was hot and heavy, as you've spent more time together it might be slipping into a routine. Although to a new couple, "routine sex" is almost comforting the first few times you have it, beware! Routine = Rut = Boredom = Time to take action and put the passion back in your relationship. When a couple's sex life is good, it seems to account for only 10 percent of the relationship, but when it's bad—it's 100 percent the focus of the relationship. Spend more time thinking about what you're going to wear to bed and less time worrying about what you're wearing out. Look hot for your man in the bedroom—think more along the lines of Frederick, Victoria and Trashy Lingerie—and less Prada and Gucci...A sexy teddy will get (and keep) your guy's attention a lot better than a new handbag!

6. Keep enjoying life! Unlike an orgasm, you can't fake this (not that you'd fake an orgasm). If you're bored, you'll be boring. He'll see it in your posture, your voice, your daily schedule. The more interests you take and the more your express your zest for life, the more contagious that energy will be. All that equals confidence, allure and attraction. It's very easy for women in new relationships that are going well to let everything else, including their girlfriends or other interests go. Don't make this mistake! Men don't want a woman who doesn't have her own interests or life.

> *Sex without love is an empty experience. But as empty experiences go, it's one of the best.*
>
> —Woody Allen

7. Don't become presumptuous about his money. In a new relationship, a man might wine and dine you at the best places in town, and buy you gifts for no reason. This is called courtship, and it's wonderful. But when your dating life slips into a more committed phase, he may see you more as "potential wife" material. This is the phase where he wants to see you in "real life"…and this is not the time to pout about all the fancy places you used to go. Don't book ritzy dinners and spa dates and expect him to pay, unless he asks you. Money issues more often than not cause tension in a relationship. Every time you are tempted to urge him to spend money on you, ask yourself, "What's more important—that ritzy restaurant or vacation, or him?" The choice should be clear.

Not only is being presumptuous with his money bad manners, it robs him of the opportunity to be the one to do these things for you, and garner your praise. Remember? He wants to feel like the hunter bringing home the catch. Don't assume—let him surprise you and feel your gratitude.

8. Change it up! The same old thing gets boring to anyone! Change up what you guys eat, change up your activities, and definitely change it up in the bedroom—start by moving the bed to a new place in the room, and get your next idea from that vantage point! Variety is the zest of life, and moving energy around shows you new ways to look at things.

9. Research and plan ahead. When planning a trip together or even his birthday party, put some effort into. Research what he'd like most and spend time putting it together for him. Make it into an interesting project for you. The joy you spend pulling this labor of love together will be evident to him, and will make him feel like he has a prize in you.

10. Most of all, remember that none of this should be work…this should be the great part of your life. You don't want to yo yo in your life like some women do with a diet. You want to incorporate these changes into a romantic and sexually charged lifestyle. Remember that the love you take it equal to the love you make. Give of yourself and you will get it back.

INTERESTING STATISTICS:

According to **E-Poll-Bridge Entertainment, Inc.'s** 2003 survey of 1,007 respondents:
There's definitely cheatin' going on! This study shows 29% of those surveyed reported having an affair, while 40% said they've had an unfaithful partner. A majority (54%) of those polled think that *men and women are equally likely to be unfaithful.* However, 43% think men are most likely to stray, and 3% think that women are most likely to be guilty of infidelity.

Most sexual activity outside a marriage or committed relationship is considered crossing the line of infidelity. The vast majority of respondents strongly agreed that *intercourse, oral sex* (91% & 89% respectively), and *fondling another man/woman* (83%) while in a committed relationship, all cross the line of infidelity. Over half of the respondents strongly agreed that *kissing another man/woman* (60%) is also an act of being unfaithful. Only 41% strongly agreed that *holding hands with another man/woman* would qualify. Women were significantly more likely than men to agree strongly that
these actions qualifies as infidelity. (ie: kissing—70% of women vs. only 51% of men.) This is also true for married respondents and those living with someone compared to those who were single, divorced or separated.

You don't have to have physical contact to cheat. Over half of respondents strongly agree that *telephone sex* (58%) and *cyber sex* (53%) would also constitute infidelity. Again, women were much more likely to consider these actions cheating (cyber sex—64% of women vs. 42% of men and telephone sex—69% of women vs. 48% of men).

Overview
In fact, fewer women said they would take their spouse/partner back if the relationship involved a *relationship over the phone or internet* (40%) compared to over half of men (average of about 54%). Those who said they have been unfaithful to a spouse/partner in the past were less likely to consider *cyber sex, telephone sex, flirting, or fantasizing about sex with others* to be "acts of infidelity" compared to those who said they have never been unfaithful.

Why do they cheat? Those who admit to being unfaithful cite the following as the top reasons for their infidelity:

Among Women:
Loneliness (22%)
To prove that they are still sexy/attractive to others (13%)
Revenge (9%)
Wanted to end my committed relationship (9%)

Among Men:
Presented with the perfect opportunity (22%)
Not getting enough sex (21%)
To prove that they are still sexy/attractive to others (9%)
Loneliness (9%)

Infidelity could be in our genes. Of those who had been unfaithful to their spouse/partner, 40% had a family history of infidelity—twice as many as those who did not have any family history (18%).

Do you want to know? About one-third of respondents say they would not want to know if their spouse/partner had a *one-night stand with someone else* (33% of men & 32% of women). About one-quarter (27% of men and 20% of women) would rather not know if their spouse/partner had a *longer-term relationship that involved sex with someone else.* Single respondents are significantly more likely to want to know if their partner is unfaithful (85%) compared to married people (74%).

After an infidelity, do you stay in a relationship or throw him/her out? When asked if they would take an unfaithful spouse/partner back, 28% of the respondents said that they *would not* take their partner back under ANY circumstances. 66% said they would *possibly* take their cheating spouse/partner back, depending on circumstances. Which gender is more forgiving? Men are more likely to take back a straying lover—69% versus 63% for women. Can you say "doormat"? 6% of the respondents *would* take back their unfaithful partner regardless of the circumstances. Men were more likely to take them back under this circumstance. Those who had been unfaithful to a spouse/partner in the past are more likely to say that they would consider taking back an unfaithful partner.

As mentioned earlier, 29% of the respondents have been unfaithful to a spouse/partner. About half of these *"unfaithfuls"* (52%) claimed that the affair *did not end* their primary relationship because their spouse/partner *never found out,* while 29% of the relationships survived after the infidelity was discovered. Only 19% of these infidelities resulted in the end of the relationship. On the other hand, among those who said they had an unfaithful spouse or partner, 67% ended their relationship.

Under what circumstances would you take your partner back?
Among those who would consider taking back their unfaithful spouse/ partner (66%), the following came in as the top reasons:
If it was a relationship that didn't involve sex (59%)
If my spouse/partner would agree to counseling afterward (51%)
If the relationship was only over the Internet (48%)
If the relationship was only over the phone (47%)

Over half of the men (average of about 54%) said that they would be more likely take their spouse/partner back if the relationship involved a *relationship over the phone or internet* compared to only 40% of women. Almost 60% claimed that the fact that their family/friends knew about the infidelity would have no effect in their willingness to take their unfaithful spouse/partner back, while 37% claimed they *would be less willing.* Almost 60% claimed that *if they know the other person that their spouse/ partner is having an affair with,* they *would be less willing to take them back.* 40% claimed this *would not have any effect at all.*

Interestingly, nearly one-quarter of males (23%) said that they would take back their spouse/partner if *they were unfaithful with a person of the same sex,* compared to only 6% of females.

© E-Poll / Bridge Entertainment, Inc. All Rights Reserved.

BONUS: The Top 10 Valentines' Day Gifts to Give Him

1. Yourself, obviously. Wrapped up in red velvet lingerie.

2. Boudoir photos of yourself.

3. If you've been dating long enough, send a thank you note to his mother and father.

4. A watch with a sexy engraving and the date on the back.

5. Have his car detailed

6. Make him an incredible dinner at home with you for dessert

7. Tell him you'd like to go to the theater or the symphony, and afterwards, while you're having drinks, slip him a hotel room key for a nearby hotel where you've made a reservation for the night.

8. Basketball tickets for the two of you

9. Arrange for two professional massages at your home to give you both massages. After the professionals leave, you continue where they left off...

10. Surprise him with a striptease, but go all out with the pole, the music, and the costume. Stop by a trashy lingerie store and get decked out for the big night in.

16

Where To Meet Successful Men

Come out come out wherever you are!

Successful men are not so abundant that you're going to trip over them on your way to the market or the gym. Think about it. The reason that they're successful is that they work long, hard hours. For instance, if they're on the west coast and they work in finance, they're probably at the office when Wall Street in New York opens—that's at 5am. The free time that these men have is precious, and they are careful about how they spend it. Your greatest opportunity to meet these busy guys lies in knowing how they spend their time and then putting yourself in a position to be "in the right place, at the right time."

A wise man once said, "90 percent of success is showing up." Well, your strategy for meeting the man of your dreams should be similarly oriented. Take control of your dating life, create new opportunities, and follow through by crafting and creating situations that make meeting successful men almost as simple and easy as just showing up!

To that end, think about this: People feel in sync with those who are like them. Like-minded folks fall into rapport very quickly. Instead of opposites attracting, "like" attracts "like." If you participate in activities that men love, you will generate the opportunity to not just meet them, but also to have an instant rapport with them.

Between men and women there is no friendship possible. There is passion, enmity, worship, love, but no friendship.
—Oscar Wilde

Where they are is where you'll want to be

The Office—Successful men work. If you happen to work in a law firm or a business where there are successful, single men, don't hesitate to use work as a resource. While you have to be more careful to avoid office politics and job interference, most people meet their boyfriends and girlfriends at work. That said if you don't work at one of these companies, but you have a friend who does, stop at her office regularly to pick her up for lunch! Get there early, and wait for her. While you're waiting, keep your eyes open, and your smile ready.

Company Christmas Parties—These celebrations are rituals, and big companies often go all out on these bashes. Get yourself invited! It isn't that difficult. If you already have friends who work at the company, then ask them to invite you. If you don't, call the Customer Service or Public Relations department, and ask them for an invitation. When you do go, don't arrive hours late. There is always a contingent of employees who uses the company Christmas party as a high-class frat party and gets wasted. You don't want to be around those people. You do want to go early in the party, and stay for an hour. Scope out anyone who looks interesting, and make yourself available.

Sports—Golf courses are man magnets. You will find successful men at every tee. Take lessons. Go with a friend. And once there, ask for help. Country clubs and exclusive sports clubs are also great venues for meeting successful men. Try going early in the morning. At six a.m. you'll catch the guys who want a work out before work. If you go regularly at the same time, you will have made yourself available. Hire a personal trainer to work with you at the club, and ask him about different men you're interested in. The trainer will have the low down, and may even make introductions.

If you live near the coast, and more specifically, near the beach, go to the beach that is adjacent to expensive real estate. Successful men will be jogging early in the morning. Many of them surf, and some of them swim before work. If you have a dog, and dogs are allowed on your beach, take your dog for a run with you. Men borrow babies for female bait—you can use your pooch for man bait.

Boating—Men love boats. Hang out at the wharf, at the boat club or even sign up for sailing lessons.

Spectator Sports—Successful men will be sitting in the good seats. Forget about nosebleed seats. You won't meet anyone but the paramedic bringing you smelling salts for the thin atmosphere. Get the best seats. You won't be wasting your time. Basketball games, tennis matches and baseball games are all great places to meet successful men. Find out if the best seats are on the floor, or in a skybox and make sure you're sitting there! If you can't buy your seats, or if they're all subscription seats, and already sold out, ask around! Lots of times big corporations have seats for the company, and your accountant or someone who works for you may have access to the seats. Ask! If you know someone who has the seats, ask them to let you know if they're ever not using them. Lots of fundraisers for charity often sell great seats at silent auctions. Bid on them. When you find yourself seated next to someone successful and interesting at one of these events, you don't want to seem too available, but it's perfectly reasonable to ask them to clarify a referee's call for you, or explain a rule. Making yourself available and open is important.

> *Men always want to be a woman's first love. That is their clumsy vanity. We women have a more subtle instinct about things. What (women) like is to be a man's last romance.*
> —Oscar Wilde

Fly First Class—Flying first class is the most wonderful way to meet a successful man. In fact, any two, three, four or five hour flight in first class, seated next to a successful man, practically counts as a first date! Cocktails, dinner and a movie are involved, so why not? If the cost of a first class ticket is prohibitive, there are lots of ways to get them. Frequent flyer mile points is the cheapest way to obtain a first class ticket or upgrade, although there are lots of rules and regulations. Many airlines will sell you an upgrade for a nominal fee from $100 to a few hundred dollars. Some airlines even offer this service at check in. Well worth the price. Make sure that you ask the airline attendant who is assigning your seat to seat you next to anyone he or she thinks is successful and attractive. While they may not know if the man is single or not, it sure doesn't hurt to ask. Also wonderful venues are members-only airport lounges. The membership fee is often under $100, and well worth the price for the company you'll get to keep and the men you'll get to meet.

Do lunch—But not dinner. You've heard it before—'power lunch.' Well there's a reason it's called that...powerful men do business with each other over lunch in restaurants. Capitalize on it! Do a little research and find out which restaurants cater to upscale businessmen in your town and then start going to them at lunch. Hey, I'll give you a hint: they are not going to be restaurants that specialize in tea and scones with crust-less sandwiches. Men like meat.

Expensive bars—The ones that are near business outlets are great places to meet men. Men often meet a buddy for a drink after work, and Happy Hour is a great time to find successful men catching a quick drink and a snack before going back to work late in the office. Happy hour is also a time when successful men will be more aware of who's in the room, since hors d'oeurves are often served at a table away from the bar, so everyone who snacks has to travel across the room and serve themselves. Don't go to expensive bars looking to meet successful men late at night. Successful men don't stay out late at night in bars—especially on week-nights. They either work late or they get their sleep, and they get up early.

> *The meeting of two personalities is like the contact of two chemical substances. If there is any reaction, both are transformed.*
>
> —Carl Jung

Online Dating—Make sure you are either using a dating service that specifies wealthy, successful men, or else make sure that you are specific in what you are looking for, to weed out anyone who is not successful. Don't waste time on men who aren't right.

Political Events—Great places to meet successful men are political events. Expensive fundraisers that are either sit down dinners or walk around cocktail parties, where you can circulate and increase your exposure, are great ways to meet men who are successful, socially active and politically involved. You also have the event at hand to automatically talk about.

Charity Events—Do something good while making yourself available. Attend a charity fundraising event. You'll increase your odds of meeting a successful, straight man by attending a fundraiser that doesn't involve AIDS or breast cancer.

Cigar Clubs—Also great places to meet successful men, as long as you don't mind smoke!

Single Parent's Kids Events—Don't forget that successful single dads take their children to Little League, T-Ball and School Open House. Whether you're a single mom, or just know one who can take you along to one of these events, you'll find some terrific men. School fundraisers—especially private school fundraisers are great places to meet these successful, single dads. Also wealthy single fathers of daughters will be clothes shopping for their little princesses at boutique kids' clothing stores in upscale malls on Saturdays. Go buy your girlfriend's kid a present—and you may meet a great single dad shopping with his daughter.

Expensive Department Stores—Shop in the men's department at a top-notch department store like Neiman's or Barney's or Saks. Buy your father or your brother in law a sweater and ask for help when you see a single guy buying a great, expensive suit. Many successful men end up dating or marrying saleswomen in these stores, so if you already work there, get to work! And if you don't work there, go get a credit card!

The Expensive Book Store Right Next to the Expensive Department Store—Beautiful independent bookstores attract successful men who like to read. Less so are the super-bookstores that carry lots of paperbacks a good bet. Instead, make your way over to the specialized stores either next to Barney's (or Neiman's or Saks) or in an expensive neighborhood, where the owner knows all the clients and customers, and can guide your or make introductions if you're a regular. Which…you need to become!

Now that you know where to go, remember everything that mantra I told you about: Enchantress, seductress, vixen, manslayer, enticer…Look good and accentuate one great feature. If you have great legs, show them off. If you have great boobs, show them off. But don't emphasize legs and breasts—you'll give the wrong message! Make your killer first impression, and smile. Use that flirtatious eye contact, and if he speaks to you, don't be shy. Play with your straw. Look at him, then look away, and look back again with a smile. Let him know you're open to a conversation, without going over to him. Make him come to you.

Summary

In the end…IT'S ALL UP TO YOU!

Think & Date Like A Man is about producing results—quickly and effectively. If it has an attitude—or if I have an attitude—it is because I believe that "attitude" is everything. It is the biggest determiner of one's success or failure, as well as the biggest contributor to, or detractor of, confidence. Change your attitude. Change your life!

No one can change your life, though, except for you. Equally, no one limits you in this life except for you. Not your parents who didn't nurture you enough, not your boss who is too hard on you, and not your third grade teacher who yelled at you in front of the class for not having your homework.

No, we cannot change our past, and we cannot change the fact that people will act in a certain way, nor can we change the inevitable…but each new day offers us the opportunity to start again, and a chance to shape our future.

And while it is true that only you can change your life, Think & Date Like A Man can assist you in that process. The book is essentially a crash-course that offers a formula for success and a method for evoking positive change. It inspires you to be the best you can be, while pursuing and successfully achieving the results you really want. Asking you the focus-driven questions to get you on the path, this book provides clear, no-nonsense answers and guidance that will insure your progression in the right direction.

Action/reaction
It's been over 2,000 years since Socrates explained "The Law of Cause and Effect," and after all this time, it still holds true. When we repeat the causes, we get the same effects. When you pick the action, you pick the result. Things do not happen by accident. Not success and not failure. Everything really does happen for reason—and that reason is you!

Success Is a Determined Action Away
The foolish with all their other thoughts, have this one too:
They are always getting ready to live, but never living.
Your success will start when you begin to pursue it.
To reach your goal or to attain success,
you don't need to know all the answers in advance.
You just need to have a clear idea of what your goal is.
Don't procrastinate when faced with a difficult problem.
Break your problems into parts
and handle one part at a time.
Develop tendencies toward taking action.
You can make something happen now.
Break your big plan into small steps and
take that first step right away.
Everyone who ever got where they are
had to begin where they were.
Your big opportunity is where you are right now.
A journey of a thousand miles begins with one step.
Take it.

—Max Stein

978-0-595-37466-3
0-595-37466-2

CPSIA information can be obtained at www.ICGtesting.com
Printed in the USA
LVOW050718130812

293959LV00001B/6/A